Salvation

Salvation

Full and Free in Christ

Banner Mini-Guides
Key Truths

Ian Hamilton

THE BANNER OF TRUTH TRUST

THE BANNER OF TRUTH TRUST
3 Murrayfield Road, Edinburgh EH12 6EL, UK
P.O. Box 621, Carlisle, PA 17013, USA

*

© The Banner of Truth Trust, 2018

ISBN
Print: 978 1 84871 806 7
EPUB: 978 1 84871 807 4
Kindle: 978 1 84871 808 1

*

Typeset in 10/14 pt Minion Pro
at the Banner of Truth Trust, Edinburgh

Printed in the USA by
Versa Press, Inc.,
East Peoria, IL

To

JOAN

the best of wives

and

my very best friend

Contents

Introduction:
God's Glorious Salvation

The Christian faith is centred on the angel's announcement to Joseph that the son conceived in Mary's womb by the power of the Holy Spirit was to be called 'Jesus', 'for he will save his people from their sins' (Matt. 1:21). The Bible is God's written revelation detailing the great salvation Jesus accomplished for everyone who would ever believe in him. By his sinless life, his sin-atoning death, and his resurrection from the dead, Jesus accomplished the salvation that no human being, however devout, could achieve. Joining himself to our frail flesh, mysteriously yet gloriously, in the womb of the Virgin Mary, God's own Son entered our fallen, broken, sin-shrouded world, to do for this world what it could never do for itself.

The following brief chapters seek to unpack this 'great salvation' (Heb. 2:3) that is found in the Lord Jesus Christ.

Of course, a book of this size cannot possibly treat this wonderful subject in much detail. It is a 'mini-guide', one of a series that will introduce the reader to some of the major themes and issues related to the Christian faith.

Each one will provide an outline of the Bible's teaching on a particular subject. They will open up a key verse or portion of Scripture for study, while not neglecting other passages related to the theme under consideration. The goal is to whet your appetite and to encourage you to explore the subject in more detail: hence the suggestions for further reading which appear after the final chapter. However, the mini-guide will provide enough information to enlarge your understanding of the theme.

All the mini-guides have been arranged in a thirteen-chapter format so that they will seamlessly fit into the teaching quarters of the church year and be useful for Sunday School lessons or Bible class studies.

My aim in writing this little book is not to set out a comprehensive doctrine of salvation, but to provide an introduction that will lead you on to explore the inexhaustible riches of grace and love that are to be found in the now risen, ascended, and glorified Son of God, Jesus Christ, who is himself the salvation of God.

IAN HAMILTON
October 2017

1

Salvation Revealed:
The Bible Alone

Today's evangelical church has its roots in the six-teenth-century Reformation. At the heart of the Protestant Reformation was the rediscovery of five foundational, biblical truths that rescued the church from its sleep of death and brought it into the sunshine of God's grace and love in Jesus Christ:

Sola scriptura (the church and the Christian's final authority is God's word, not the traditions of the church);

Sola gratia (salvation is by God's free, unmerited mercy, not by our initiative or deserving);

Sola fides (we enter into the salvation won by Jesus Christ by faith alone, not by any contribution we can make);

Solus Christus (Jesus Christ alone secures salvation for sinners, not the sacraments of the church or the priestly intercession of the church);

Soli Deo gloria (the glory, all of it, belongs to God alone). The great truth that inspired men such as Martin Luther and John Calvin to stand courageously against the worship, life, and doctrine of the Roman Catholic Church was that Holy Scripture, the word of God, alone was the Christian's and the church's ultimate and final authority. Their watchword was, 'To the teaching and to the testimony! If they will not speak according to this word, it is because they have no dawn' (Isa. 8:20).

In this opening chapter we will briefly consider what is meant by *sola scriptura* and how vital it is for the church today to rediscover the authority, sufficiency, grace, and truth of God's word.

First, we need to understand what *sola scriptura* is not. By 'Scripture alone', Martin Luther, John Calvin, Thomas Cranmer, John Knox, and the whole Reformation movement did not mean *nuda scriptura*, that is, Scripture with no reference at all to the church's tradition. In teaching and preaching *sola scriptura*, the reformers were not saying that all tradition was bad. They all believed in tradition. They did not believe that every man and woman should interpret God's word apart from the creeds or the teaching ministry of the church throughout its history. They did not mean that the individual Christian was a little pope who, with the Bible in hand, could ignore the church and think and live as he or she pleased. The reformers were acutely aware of the sinful exaltation of private judgment. They understood that it is only 'with all the saints' that we can begin to comprehend 'what is the breadth and length and height and depth' of Christ's love (Eph. 3:18-19).

Nor does *sola scriptura* mean that God's revelation of himself in creation amounts to nothing. Creation reveals something true and real about God (Psa. 19:1; Rom. 1:19-20). Yet it is possible to carefully study God's creation but never grasp that God is holy. You can watch a glorious sunset and never know that God hates sin. You can gaze through the Hubble telescope and never know that each one of us stands under God's just judgment. You can dissect a fruit-fly and penetrate into subatomic particles and never realize that you can never work your way into God's friendship, that you are incapable of making amends for your sin or fitting yourself for God's holy presence. God's revelation in creation is not a saving revelation.

There is something else: *sola scriptura* does not mean God's word apart from God's Spirit. John Calvin famously likened God's word to spectacles; but what good are spectacles to someone who is blind? The person needs new eyes to see through the spectacles. Calvin proceeded to speak of the necessity of the ministry of the Holy Spirit in the new birth, enabling us to 'see' (John 3:3). John Owen, the great English Puritan, put this memorably when he wrote: 'he that would utterly separate the Spirit from the word had as good burn his Bible. The bare letter of the New Testament will no more ingenerate faith and obedience in the souls of men ... than the letter of the Old Testament.'[1] In saying this, Owen is echoing what Paul plainly states in 1 Corinthians 2:14: 'The natural person does not accept

---

[1] John Owen, *Works* (London: Banner of Truth Trust, 1966), III:192.

the things of the Spirit of God, for they are folly to him, and he is not able to understand them because they are spiritually discerned.'

What then does *sola scriptura* mean? The cry 'No book but the Bible' has invariably been that of heretics throughout the ages. But simply to affirm a string of texts from the Bible begs the question, 'But what do these texts mean?'

Sola scriptura means that God has revealed himself, his way of salvation and how he is to be served and worshipped alone, in his Spirit-inspired word. All human thoughts, speech, and writing must therefore be examined in the light of God's infallible word (Isa. 8:20). God's written word is the church's and the Christian's infallible touchstone. Since 'all Scripture is breathed out by God' (2 Tim. 3:16), it is absolutely trustworthy and reliable. It is described as a 'lamp shining in a dark place' (2 Pet. 1:19), a lamp to our feet and a light to our path (Psa. 119:105). It is this breathed-out word of God alone that makes us 'wise for salvation through faith in Christ Jesus' (2 Tim. 3:15).

What then has God revealed to us in his word that he has not revealed to us in creation or conscience? Five things in particular.

1. *Who he is*

In Exodus 33:18 Moses asked the Lord to show him his glory. The Lord's response to Moses was a stunning self-disclosure of his character: 'The LORD passed before him and proclaimed, "The LORD, the LORD, a God merciful and gracious, slow to anger, and abounding in steadfast love and faithfulness, keeping steadfast love for thousands, forgiving iniquity and transgression and sin, but who will by no means clear the guilty, visiting the iniquity of the fathers on the children and the children's children, to the third and the fourth generation'" (Exod. 34:6-7). Who would ever have imagined that the Almighty Creator of all things was such a God? Gazing endlessly at the wonders of creation would never have unlocked to us the heart of God. More wonderfully, the eternal God has come in the person of his Son and made himself known (John 1:1-3, 14, 18). But we only know this because 'the Bible tells us so'. If we did not have the God-breathed Bible (2 Tim. 3:16), our knowledge of God would be pure conjecture.

2. *Who we are*

It is commonplace in our modern day to believe that human beings are evolutionary accidents. In the Bible, which is God's infallibly true revelation, we discover what we intuitively know, that we are not evolutionary accidents; rather, we are those who have been 'fearfully and wonderfully made' (Psa. 139:14). The innate dignity of every human being is placarded on the first page of the Bible: 'Then God said, "Let us make man in our image, after our likeness …" So God created man in his own image, in the image of God he created him; male and female he created them' (Gen. 1:26-27). God's word unambiguously proclaims the equal dignity of men and women irrespective of race or culture or education. We possess dignity not because of our history or heritage or education or perceived value to society, but because the Creator of all things made us in his image and likeness.

3. *God's way of salvation in Jesus Christ his Son*

If we did not have the Bible we would be lost in a fog of ignorance. We might sense that we need to be right with God, but we would have no clue as to how that might be. But God has spoken. He has given us his word to make us 'wise for salvation through faith in Christ Jesus' (2 Tim. 3:15; John 14:6; 3:16). In the Bible God shows us why we need his salvation and what he has done in his incarnate Son to save us and restore us to his friendship and fellowship. Before it is anything else, the Bible is God's 'handbook of salvation'. In the Bible God reveals why we need his salvation in Jesus Christ and what he has done in Christ to save sinners. In the Bible we discover that we can never earn God's salvation, but that he gives it as a free gift in Christ.

4. *How God wants us to live*

The Bible is not a moral handbook, but it does spell out how God wants his forgiven, saved children to live (Psa. 119:105; 2 Tim. 3:16-17; Matt. 28:19-20). It is remarkable to notice in the Bible that all of God's commands are embedded in his prior grace. Obedience to God's commands is never coldly or clinically demanded. The summons to obedience is always rooted in God's love and grace. We see this memorably in the Ten Commandments. Before the Lord details how he desires his covenant people to live, he says, 'I am the LORD your God, who brought you out of the land of Egypt, out of the house of slavery' (Exod. 20:2). Love makes obedience truly sweet.

5. *How God wants us to worship him*

In 1543 John Calvin wrote a small treatise entitled *The Necessity of Reforming the Church*. He had been urged by his friend Martin Bucer to explain to the Emperor Charles V why the Christian church needed to be reformed. What Calvin wrote in this brilliant little book highlights the reformers' conviction of the relationship between the worship of God and the word of God:

> If it be inquired, then, by what things chiefly the Christian religion has a standing existence amongst us and maintains its truth, it will be found that the following two not only occupy the principal place, but comprehend under them all the other parts, and consequently the whole substance of Christianity, viz., a knowledge, first, of the mode in which God is duly worshipped; and, secondly of the source from which salvation is to be obtained.

The first concern of all the reformers was a knowledge of the mode in which God is duly worshipped and the second, a knowledge of the source from which salvation is to be obtained. It is somewhat artificial to separate these two: you cannot worship God as he has commanded until you are born again and brought by the God of grace into a right relationship with himself. But the reformers were persuaded that God has as much revealed in his word how he is to be worshipped as he has the way of salvation by faith alone, in Jesus Christ alone.

Calvin saw that much of what passed for the worship of God was little more than fabricated ideas formed with little or no reference to Holy Scripture. He could have been speaking for our day when he wrote:

> I know how difficult it is to persuade the world that God disapproves of all modes of worship not expressly sanctioned by his word. The opposite persuasion which cleaves to them, being seated, as it were, in their very bones and marrow, is, that whatever they do has in itself a sufficient sanction, provided it exhibits some kind of zeal for the honour of God.

Similarly, in his response to Cardinal Sadoleto's letter pleading with Geneva to abandon the Reformation and return to the Roman Catholic Church, Calvin said: 'There is nothing more perilous to our salvation than a preposterous and perverse worship of God.'[1]

It is strange that many Christians today should be so passionate in defending and contending for the biblical truth of justification by grace alone, through faith alone, in Christ alone, and yet be so indifferent to the biblical truth that God is to be worshipped according to his word and not according to our fertile imaginations. Think for a moment of the solemn judgment that fell on Nadab and Abihu (Lev. 10:1-2).

---

[1] John Calvin, *Tracts and Letters* (Edinburgh: Banner of Truth Trust, 2009), I:34.

Jesus' temptations: a case study in biblical authority

Jesus' temptations were real. They came to him when he was physically and mentally weak (Matt. 4:2). They came at a critical time in his ministry, immediately after his baptism when he identified himself with sinners and committed himself to the mission given to him by his Father. How did Jesus respond? Three times he responded to the devil's temptations by quoting from the word of God (Matt. 4:4, 7, 10). Jesus had such absolute confidence in God's word that he used it to repulse the 'flaming darts of the evil one' (Eph. 6:16). For Jesus it was enough to say, 'It is written …' In saying this, Jesus was not worshipping a book; he was acknowledging that Scripture was the written word of the God who cannot lie.

John Calvin understood this truth; he wrote: 'we owe to the Scripture the same reverence that we owe to God; because it has proceeded from him alone, and has nothing belonging to man mixed with it'.[1]

In his threefold response to the devil's temptations, Jesus confessed his confidence in the intrinsic authority of God's word, the unconditional sufficiency of God's word, and the ever-relevant wisdom of God's word. He is our example and model. We are to have the same confidence in the word of God as he had. 'It is written.' This is where Christians cast their anchor in the midst of life's trials and temptations because this is where our Lord Jesus cast his anchor!

---

[1] John Calvin, *Commentaries on the Epistles to Timothy, Titus, and Philemon* (Edinburgh: Calvin Translation Society, 1856), 2 Tim. 3:16.

John Wesley, the famous eighteenth-century evangelist, wrote:

I have thought, I am a creature of a day, passing through life as an arrow through the air. I am a spirit come from God, and returning to God: just hovering over the great gulf; till a few moments hence, I am no more seen! I drop into an unchangeable eternity! I want to know one thing, the way to heaven: how to land safe on that happy shore. God himself has condescended to teach the way; for this very end he came from heaven. He hath written it down in a book! O give me that book! At any price, give me the book of God! I have it: here is knowledge enough for me. Let me be *homo unius libri*.[1]

[1] Latin: a man of one book. 'Mr Wesley's Preface to the Sermons', in *Works of the Reverend John Wesley*, 7 vols. (New York: J. Emory and B. Waugh, 1831), I:xix.

2

The Roots of Salvation:
God's Covenant of Redemption

The Bible is insistent that 'salvation is of the Lord'. Salvation from beginning to end is the purpose and prerogative of God. We are helpless to save ourselves. Sin has completely disabled us spiritually. We can no more save ourselves than fly to the sun on wings of wax. If salvation in all its aspects were not 'of the Lord', no one would be saved. Paul reminds the church in Ephesus that before God had made them 'alive with Christ', they were 'dead in trespasses and sins', children of God's wrath, 'without hope and without God'. This dark and depressing picture of men and women without Christ is why the New Testament likens salvation to a resurrection from the dead. Without God giving us new life, we would never turn to Christ and embrace him as Saviour and Lord. Salvation truly is of the Lord.

What we need to understand is precisely what this phrase 'of the Lord' means. It certainly means that apart from the Lord's gracious and sovereign initiative no one could or would be saved. But the phrase means more than that. It means that the Lord in the tri-unity of his being is Saviour. Not the Father only. Not the Son only. Not the Holy Spirit only. Salvation is the concerted purpose and achievement of Father, Son and Holy Spirit.

The Bible never presents any one person of the Holy Trinity exclusively as Saviour. Certainly it was the Son of God, Jesus Christ, and not the Father who died as a sin-atoning Saviour on the cross. It was the Son and not the Father who died 'the righteous for the unrighteous, that he might bring us to God' (1 Pet. 3:18). But the Son who died, died as the Servant of the Lord, in obedience to his Father's will. And he did so upheld by the eternal Spirit (Heb. 9:14). Salvation is the agreed purpose and provision of the Holy Trinity.

This is a truth that is embedded in the Bible's unfolding drama of salvation. In times eternal, Father, Son and Holy Spirit covenanted to save a people to God's endless praise.

With this in mind, it is striking to notice that every phase of our Saviour's life was shaped and styled by his self-conscious sense that he had come from heaven 'not to do [his] own will but the will of him who sent [him]' (John 6:38). Indeed, it would not be over-stretching the point to say that John 6:37-40 is programmatic of the whole course of Jesus' life of covenant obedience to his Father. There he stands before us not as a private individual but as the appointed covenant head of God's elect. It is as the one appointed by God to be his Servant and his people's head that Jesus declares his self-denying obedience to the will of his Father, to the end that he should lose not one of those given to him by his Father (John 6:39).

This truth alone makes sense of everything our Lord did throughout the course of his earthly, and continues to do throughout the course of his present heavenly, life as the God-Man. All he does is for all those he represents (Rom. 5:18-19; 1 Cor. 15:22). This truth is embedded in our Lord's self-conscious sense of having been 'given' a people to save by his Father.

This holy resolve to obey his Father, whatever the cost (and it cost him everything), did not, however, begin and develop primarily within the psychology of his sinless humanity. In the councils of eternity, the Son of God, with his Father and the Spirit, conspired and decreed, in astonishing love, to create a world, and out of the sinful mass of that world, all fallen in its appointed covenant head Adam, to redeem a people, for their own glory. This covenant of redemption lies at the heart of the biblical plan of salvation and shaped the earthly, and the present heavenly, life of our Saviour. The effect of this covenant was that Christ, by fulfilling the terms of the covenant, secured all the blessings that flow to believing sinners from the covenant of grace.

It was Jesus' sense of living under the constraints of the covenant of redemption that profoundly shaped the whole course of his earthly mission.

First, it measured the pace of his mission. The whole course of his earthly mission was directed by a divinely devised timetable. The marked self-consciousness of living in obedient servanthood to his Father reveals itself in a significant way throughout John's Gospel. Again and again we find our Lord shaping his earthly agenda not by the circumstances of the moment, but by the realization that the dominating, controlling motif in his life was a 'decreed hour'. At the wedding in Cana, he tells his mother who is expecting him to remedy, in some way, the lack of wine, 'My hour has not yet come' (John 2:4). Later as the shadow of the cross begins to penetrate his soul, he declares, 'Now is my soul troubled. And what shall I say? "Father, save me from this hour"? But for this purpose I have come to this hour. Father glorify your name' (John 12:27-28a). This led to Jesus at times strategically withdrawing from confrontation with his enemies. He was never motivated by cowardice, but always by a submissive obedience to the decreed timetable of his Father. Every step of the way Jesus knew that his times were in his Father's hands.

This truth ought no less to measure the pace of the believer's life. Our times are also in God's hands. Even with our different temperaments and personalities, should not our lives betray that truth? The predestinarian character of biblical religion ought, above all else, to give our lives a sense of poise and unruffled assurance, even when all around us others are losing their heads.

Second, it moulded the character of his mission. Jesus had come to be God's 'obedient Servant' and he avoided no necessary cost in fulfilling the willingly received commission given to him by his Father. We see Jesus, as the perfect image of the Father (John 14:9), insisting on the costly career of inflexible obedience to his Father's word. Nowhere is this more movingly described for us than in his agony in the garden and in its immediate aftermath. Mark tells us, he 'began to be greatly distressed and troubled'. He told Peter, James and John, 'My soul is very sorrowful, even to death.' And yet he embraces the cup his Father had prepared for him, the cup he had committed himself to drinking when the triune God devised the covenant of redemption. The terms of the covenant constrained our beloved Saviour to walk the way of inflexible, but ever willingly given, obedience.

Never imagine that it was effortless for our Lord Jesus to walk that way. Obedience to his Father cost him everything! For him there was no other way to live. He was living out the obedience he had promised to give to his Father in times eternal. Faithfulness to his Father required it; the salvation of God's elect depended on it. The Saviour's servanthood was therefore a covenantal servanthood. Nothing less would secure God's decreed salvation for all his people.

Third, it motivated the spirit of his earthly mission. He had come from the Father as his Servant. He delighted to offer to the Father the covenant obedience to which he pledged himself in the eternal council—'I delight to do your will, O God'. The fact that he was acting in obedience to his Father's will in fulfilling all the conditions of the covenant of redemption drew from our Lord Jesus the motivating spirit that rendered his obedience pleasing to his Father. There was nothing forced or grudging or reluctant about

Jesus' obedience. So much so, that the Father split the heavens to say, 'You are my beloved Son; with you I am well pleased' (Mark 1:11).

In our Lord Jesus' life we see the pre-eminent value of 'heart' obedience. We can never be reminded too often that our God looks on the heart. It is only too easy to drift into mindless, mechanical, clinical servanthood. As the Father's Servant-King, our Saviour lived *coram deo* (before the face of God). This is the essence of biblical piety. This is why we read again and again throughout the Old Testament that the most meticulous performance of God-ordained ritual cannot begin to compensate for the absence of heart-worship and love: 'the sacrifices of God are a broken spirit; a broken and contrite heart, O God, you will not despise' (Psa. 51:17; cf. Isa. 1:10ff.).

Fourth, it inspired the unruffled confidence that impregnated his earthly mission (cf. John 6:37, 39, 40). Our Servant-King never wavered in the execution of his office, as was prophesied of him in Isaiah 42:3. Never was our Lord for one moment uncertain about the outcome of his mission. This assurance meant that the whole course of his earthly life was marked by a sure, unruffled sense of what he was about and where he was going. He knew that his Father's promise to support and strengthen him by the indwelling presence and ministry of the Holy Spirit would absolutely be fulfilled. When he exhorted his disciples to be anxious about nothing because 'your heavenly Father knows', he was simply saying to them what the heavenly Father had said, as it were, to him.

This is something we all need to learn. Poiseful Christian living is not the fruit of a particular kind of temperament, but the fruit of knowing that our times are in our gracious and sovereign Lord's hands. 'The Lord is my helper; what can man do to me?' Practical, godly living is embedded in deeply understood theology. The doctrine of God, understanding who God is and his covenanted commitment to his people, breathes poise and quiet, unruffled confidence into the Christian's heart. So it did to our Lord Jesus, the proto-typical man of faith.

Fifth, it manifested the loving, merciful attitude of God that was the animating heartbeat of his earthly mission. What prompted God to send his only Son to be the Saviour of the world? In a word, 'love'. 'God so loved the world, that he gave his only Son' (John 3:16); 'God shows his love for us in that while we were still sinners, Christ died for us' (Rom. 5:8). Sovereign love to rebellious, judgment-deserving sinners was the fountain out of which redemption flowed to a lost world. It was not surprising, then, that this love was the heartbeat that animated every step of Jesus' mission. When he saw the crowds, Matthew tells us, 'he had compassion for them, because they were harassed and helpless, like sheep without a shepherd' (Matt. 9:36). When the 'rich young ruler' came to him asking, 'What must I do to inherit eternal life?', Jesus looked at him and 'loved him' (Mark 10:21). When the Pharisees expressed their disgust that he should receive sinners and eat with them(Luke 15:2), Jesus told them a series of parables culminating in the Parable of the Prodigal Son (Luke 15:11-32). In this parable, Jesus likened God to the father of the lost son, who, when he saw his repentant son returning home, was felt compassion, threw his arms around him and kissed him. The Pharisees could not understand Jesus because they did not understand that 'God is love' (1 John 4:8, 16).

Jesus' disregard for social and traditional religious conventions was due to his compassion for sinners—love for sinners made him seek, by all means, to save some. The compassion that shone through Jesus' earthly life was the overflow of the covenant of redemption. It was this love, expressed in obedience to the will of his Father, that kept Jesus on track and led him to embrace the dark, unspeakable desolation of the cross. It was our sins that held him there, but only because love was offering itself, the just for the unjust, to bring us to God.

It is a wonderful thing that the triune God should have resolved in sovereign, unfathomable grace to love a world of lost sinners and save them. He bound himself to do so and fulfilled that 'binding' when the Lord Jesus Christ made propitiation for our sins and rose in triumph over sin and death and hell. It is little wonder Paul exclaimed, 'Oh, the depth of the riches of the wisdom and knowledge of God! … For from him and through him and to him are all things. To him be glory for ever. Amen' (Rom. 11:33-36).

3

Salvation's Storyline:
The History of Redemption

The salvation God has provided for this world is presented to us in the unfolding story of Holy Scripture. This story covers the length and breadth of the Bible and is its thematic plot-line. The story begins in Genesis with the completion of creation and God's declaration as he surveyed his work, 'very good' (Gen. 1:31). But only too soon, the 'very good' of creation is dramatically spoiled by the intrusion of sin and Satan (Gen. 3). How a mere creature could wreak such havoc and bring sin and death into the perfection of God's creation is a mystery. The Bible is absolutely insistent that God ordains all things according to the counsel of his own will (Eph. 1:11). What happened in the Garden of Eden did not catch God unawares. God did not initiate Plan B in the wake of Adam's sin. He is never a passive, far less a helpless, bystander in the face of human sin and rebellion. God's promise to raise up someone from the seed of the woman to crush the serpent's head (Gen.

3:15) was no knee-jerk reaction to Adam's seduction, but his wise, thoughtful, long-ordained response to a calamity he had sovereignly and sinlessly purposed.

The whole Bible is an unfolding explanation of that first promise, 'I will put enmity between you [Satan] and the woman, and between your offspring [seed] and her offspring [seed]; he shall bruise your head, and you shall bruise his heel' (Gen. 3:15). God is personally and unequivocally promising to defeat the enemy who had initiated Adam and Eve's rebellion against their good and gracious God. The tragedy is compounded by Luke's description of Adam as 'the son of God' (Luke 3:38). Luke was not saying that Adam was '*the* Son of God', but he was telling us that Adam was no mere servant in his disobedience to God in the Garden of Eden. Adam was a son. God was his Father.

If you remember reading Genesis 3:15 for the first time, you must have wondered, 'What does this mean? Who is this offspring of the woman who will bruise the serpent's (Satan's) head, but who will himself be bruised in the process?' The promise is at this point in the story an enigma, a tantalizing puzzle. The puzzle is not solved until we come to the first page in the New Testament, the opening chapter of Matthew's Gospel. An angel of the Lord appeared to Joseph, whose betrothed, Mary, was 'with child', and said, 'Joseph, son of David, do not fear to take Mary as your wife, for that which is conceived in her is from the Holy Spirit. She will bear a son, and you shall call his name Jesus, for he will save his people from their sins' (Matt. 1:20-21). Jesus is the offspring, the seed of the woman, who had come to bruise the serpent's, Satan's, head. Jesus is the true and faithful Son who, as God's 'better-than-Adam', would destroy the devil and his works (1 John 3:8). It was for this reason he appeared (1 John 3:8).

Between Genesis 3:15 and Matthew 1:20-21, the first gospel promise is the centrepiece of the Bible's unfolding story of salvation. Step by step, slowly but surely, definition and increasing clarity is given to the promise.

Towards the close of Genesis, Jacob gathers his sons to prophesy God's purpose for each of them (Gen. 49:1). His prophetic word to Judah stands out like a beacon: 'The sceptre shall not depart from Judah, nor the ruler's staff from between his feet, until tribute comes to him; and to him shall be the obedience of the peoples' (Gen. 49:10).

Earlier in Genesis 12, God had promised Abram, '... in you all the families of the earth shall be blessed' (Gen. 12:3). Now, through Jacob's prophecy, God singles out the tribe of Judah to be the supreme focus for the realization of that promise.

Between God's promise to Abraham and the anointing of David, the Bethlehemite from Judah, one thousand years passed. Long years of waiting and wondering. When would God fulfil his promise to send the one who would crush the serpent's head? Who would he be? Now, God commanded Samuel to go to Bethlehem, 'for I have provided for myself a king among [Jesse's] sons' (1 Sam. 16:1). To Samuel's surprise, God chose the youngest son, David. Samuel had expected God to choose Eliab because of his physical stature and presence (1 Sam. 16:6). But the Lord said to Samuel, 'Do not look on his appearance or on the height of his stature, because I have rejected him. For the LORD sees not as man sees: man looks on the outward appearance, but the LORD looks on the heart' (1 Sam. 16:7).

David was Israel's greatest king; but he was deeply flawed. He arranged the murder of Uriah the Hittite in order to cover up his adultery with Bathsheba, Uriah's wife (see 2 Sam. 11). But in one telling respect, David typified God's ultimate and perfect King. Just as David was not the kind of king Samuel expected, so God's own Son, Jesus Christ, was not the kind of King anyone expected. In the fourth Servant Song in Isaiah, the prophetic description of God's coming Messiah-King is stunning: 'he had no form or majesty that we should look at him, and no beauty that we should desire him. He was despised and rejected by men; a man of sorrows, and acquainted with grief; and as one from whom men hide their faces he was despised, and we esteemed him not' (Isa. 53:2-3).

It hardly seemed credible that this was how men and women would look on God's promised King. The detail concerning this King was given more definition in the prophecy of Micah, where we are told that this God-appointed and anointed Ruler, whose origin was 'from ancient days' (Mic. 5:2), would come from Bethlehem (like David), the least of the clans of Judah (Mic. 5:2).

The climax of God's unfolding promise to send a Deliverer was reached in the birth, life, death and resurrection of Jesus Christ. Born in Bethlehem (Matt. 1:18–2:12), he lived the one perfect human life, died a God-ordained sin-atoning death, and was raised in triumph from the grave on the third day. In Jesus Christ, God's promise to send one from the seed of woman to crush the serpent came to its glorious fulfilment. The one who was crucified in weakness (2 Cor. 13:4) 'disarmed the rulers and authorities', putting them to open shame, triumphing over them by his cross (Col. 2:15).

Jesus' triumph over sin and death and Satan on the cross was the decisive moment in the history of the world. But the final demise of Satan awaits Jesus' coming again in power and in glory at the end of history. Only then will Satan be finally and forever cast into the lake of eternal fire, never again to trouble God's children (Rev. 20).

When Jesus comes again to this fallen, broken world, and inaugurates a new heaven and new earth, the home of righteousness (2 Pet. 3), then the Bible's storyline will come to its ordained conclusion. The groaning creation caused by Adam's fall (Rom. 8:18-20) will give way to the renewed creation, restored to its pristine glory and eternally secured by Jesus' triumph over sin and death and hell. So, according to God's promise, we wait expectantly for this new creation (2 Pet. 3) where there will be no more sin or sorrow or pain or fear, because God will be all in all (Rev. 21; 1 Cor. 15:28).

To many people it might seem very strange that Christians should have one boast, the cross of Christ (Gal. 6:14). The cross was a barbaric instrument of execution. And yet it was on the cross that God accomplished his promise to crush Satan and bring deliverance to his people. Yes, he was crucified in weakness; but by his resurrection, Jesus lives 'by the power of God' (2 Cor. 13:4). It is little wonder then that Paul could write, 'we preach Christ crucified' (1 Cor. 1:23). The message of the cross was, and continues to be, foolishness and weakness to the world (1 Cor. 1:23-25). To Christians, however, it is nothing less than 'the power of God and the wisdom of God' (1 Cor. 1:24).

Amidst the wreckage of the Garden of Eden, God made a promise to bruise the head of Satan, the enemy. And he did. He found in his own Son a better-than-Adam, a Servant-Son who would not flinch nor fail, who would be obedient unto death, even the death on a cross (Phil. 2:8). Truly, 'all the promises of God find their Yes in him [Christ]' (2 Cor. 1:20).

4

Salvation Breaks into Our World: The Incarnation

The New Testament makes no attempt anywhere to explain the incarnation, the in-fleshing, of the eternal Word who was with God and who was God: 'In the beginning was the Word, and the Word was with God, and the Word was God … And the Word became flesh' (John 1:1, 14). It was not that the New Testament writers were unintelligent; they were simply out of their depth. In the incarnation of his Son, God acted as only God can act. He does not act according to the limits of our rationality. Purposefully and deliberately he takes us out of our intellectual comfort zone. Our appropriate response to the incarnation should never first be intellectual curiosity but adoring wonder. In the incarnation of his Son God confronts us all with his incomprehensibility as well as with his love.

God's eternal Word became flesh

'And the Word became flesh' (John 1:14). We need to pause and try and take in the stupendous truth of these words.

They are easily parsed but not so easily understood. John is uninterested in reflecting on the metaphysics of the incarnation; the 'how' is beyond him. He simply states the bare fact of the incarnation: God's eternal Word, his ultimate self-expression, his own Son, 'became flesh'. The verb is staggering. He 'became' flesh. John doesn't mean he became a divine man! The mystery of two distinct natures in one person, 'without confusion, without change, without division, without separation' (the words are from the Creed of Chalcedon, AD 451), is an unfathomable mystery (1 Tim. 3:16). The flesh he joined to his eternal being was not a robe he put on only later to take off. He 'became' flesh. His humanity was not an illusion; he did not merely appear to be like us, he became one of us, apart from sin (Rom. 8:3; Heb. 7:26). In his Commentary on John's Gospel, Calvin daringly says that the flesh Christ 'became' was 'addicted to so many wretchednesses'. He lived in our flesh, he died in our flesh, he rose in our flesh, he reigns in our flesh and one day he will return in our flesh—glorified flesh, no longer marked by weakness, but still our flesh.

God's eternal Word dwelt among us

'… and dwelt among us'. There are two thoughts here: First, he 'dwelt' among us. More literally translated, the Greek verb means the Word *pitched his tabernacle*, or *lived in his tent*, amongst us. In the Old Testament, the tent of meeting was where God met with his people. After giving Moses detailed and intricate instructions concerning the building of the 'sanctuary' (Exod. 25:8), the Lord tells him, 'I will consecrate the tent of meeting … I will dwell among the people of Israel and will be their God' (Exod. 29:44-45; read the whole account in Exod. 25–29). God's people knew that the tent of meeting could not begin to contain God. In his prayer of dedication at the building of the temple, Solomon prayed, 'Behold, heaven and the highest heaven cannot contain you, how much less this house that I have built!' (2 Chron. 6:18). But now in the incarnation of God's own Son, the uncontainable God had come into the midst of his creation. God had come into the world in person to meet with his people.

Second, he dwelt 'among us'. Perhaps the greatest wonder of the incarnation is that the Holy One (Isa. 6:3) came in person to live 'among' the squalor, sin, darkness, and death of this world. The Lord Jesus Christ, incarnate God, lived out his sinless life among the filth of this world, not in isolation or at a distance from it.

The Christian church has always understood that its mission is to live out its life as the people of God in the midst of a fallen world, to live out the life of faith and obedience holding out the Lord Jesus Christ to a decaying and dying world (Matt. 5:13-16). When the church isolates and distances itself from the squalor, darkness, and death in the world, it repudiates its calling to be the light of the world and the salt of the earth. There may well be a sore cost to being gospel light-bearers in a fallen world, but the servant is not greater than his Master.

God's eternal Word revealed his glory:

'... and we have seen his glory, glory as of the only Son from the Father, full of grace and truth' (John 1:14). John is speaking first for himself and the other apostles; they had seen Christ's glory. John's language echoes Exodus 33–34. There Moses asked to see God's glory and the Lord said, 'I will make all my goodness pass before you ... The LORD passed before him and proclaimed, "The LORD, the LORD, a God merciful and gracious"' (34:6). The Lord wanted Moses to understand that at the heart of his glory was a 'goodness' (33:19) characterized by mercy and grace.

Many others saw what John saw but did not 'see' the glory of Jesus. They saw someone whom they despised and rejected, who had 'no form or majesty' that attracted them to him (Isa. 53:2-3). So they crucified the Lord of glory (1 Cor. 2:8). There is a hiddenness to the glory of God's incarnate Word that is only penetrated by the eye of faith. Faith 'sees' in a despised, rejected, and crucified Jesus of Nazareth, the Lamb of God who takes away the sin of the world (John 1:29).

The question that must now be asked is, *Why?* Why did the Son of God become flesh?

Why the Son of God became flesh

The incarnation of God's Son was not a naked display of God's power and glory. God sent his Son into the world to be the Saviour of the world (John 3:16; 6:33). He sent his Son to overcome the power of death and behind death its unholy master Satan. The letter to the Hebrews wonderfully captures the reasons behind the incarnation of the Son of God:

> Since therefore the children share in flesh and blood, he himself likewise partook of the same things, that through death he might destroy the one who has the power of death, that is, the devil, and deliver all those who through fear of death were subject to lifelong slavery. For surely it is not angels that he helps, but he helps the offspring of Abraham. Therefore he had to be made like his brothers in every respect, so that he might become a merciful and faithful high priest in the service of God, to make propitiation for the sins of the people. For because he himself has suffered when tempted, he is able to help those who are being tempted (Heb. 2:14-18).

While we cannot begin to understand the 'how', we can, more importantly, understand the 'why' of the incarnation. God the Son 'became flesh' (John 1:14) to do for us what we could never do for ourselves. In no other way than by becoming what we are, without sin (Heb. 7:26), could God reconcile us to himself.

But the incarnation also highlights that the God who made us and who knows us has become one with us in his Son. And in becoming one with us, Jesus is able to help us, because he knows what it is to be tempted and to suffer (Heb. 2:18). He is our 'merciful and faithful high priest' who has 'in every respect ... been tempted as we are, yet without sin' (Heb. 4:15). He knows our frame, not only by omniscient observation, but by personal experience (Psa. 103:14). Alongside his finished work of making atonement for sin, our Lord Jesus Christ has a continuing work of ministering help and comfort to those with whom he is united in a common humanity in the bond of the Holy Spirit (Heb. 2:16-17).

John Calvin memorably explained the 'why' of the incarnation:

> it was also imperative that he who was to become our Redeemer be true God and true man. It was his task to swallow up death. Who but the Life could do this? It was his task to conquer sin. Who but very righteousness could do this? It was his task to rout the powers of world and air. Who but a power higher than world and air could do this? Now where does life or righteousness or lordship and authority of heaven lie but with God alone? Therefore our most merciful God, when he willed that we be redeemed, made himself our Redeemer in the person of his only-begotten Son.[1]

More than anything else, the incarnation of the Lord Jesus Christ highlights the unfathomable love of God for his sinful, rebellious world. The eternal God who is himself uncontainable, became containable in the God-Man Jesus Christ. The sheer grace of God's love is beyond all words.

In his letter to the Philippians, Paul wrote about the unfathomable condescension of God the Son in becoming a man that he might thereby rescue us from a lost eternity and bring us into the kingdom and family of God. Remark-

---

[1] John Calvin, *Institutes of the Christian Religion*, ed. John T. McNeill, tr. Ford Lewis Battles (Philadelphia: Westminster Press, 1960), II.xii.2.

ably, Paul wrote these words in order to encourage the Philippian church to behave with humility and generosity towards one another:

> Have this mind among yourselves, which is yours in Christ Jesus, who, though he was in the form of God, did not count equality with God a thing to be grasped, but emptied himself, by taking the form of a servant, being born in the likeness of men. And being found in human form, he humbled himself by becoming obedient to the point of death, even death on a cross. Therefore God has highly exalted him and bestowed on him the name that is above every name, so that at the name of Jesus every knee should bow, in heaven and on earth and under the earth, and every tongue confess that Jesus Christ is Lord, to the glory of God the Father (Phil. 2:5-11).

Jesus Christ, the incarnate Son of God, sits even now on the throne of God. Glorified dust on the throne of the cosmos. Behold your God!

5

Salvation's Pivotal Moment: The Centrality of the Cross

The cross of Jesus Christ is the climactic centrepiece of the Christian faith. Jesus himself understood this: 'Now is my soul troubled. And what shall I say? "Father, save me from this hour"? But for this purpose I have come to this hour' (John 12:27). The apostle Paul understood the centrality of Jesus' death on the cross. To the church in Corinth he wrote, 'I decided to know nothing among you except Jesus Christ and him crucified' (1 Cor. 2:2). And to the churches in Galatia he wrote, 'far be it from me to boast except in the cross of our Lord Jesus Christ' (Gal. 6:14). If we are to make any sense of the cross of Christ, we have seen that we need to understand that 'the cross is the pulpit of God's love'.

When the New Testament speaks of the cross, it always tells us that it was the provision of the Father's love (John 3:16; 1 John 4:9-10; 2 Cor. 13:14; Rom. 5:5). In these and other texts, it is the Father's love that is highlighted. Before it is anything else, the cross is the revelation of God's love. It is no less the demonstration of his justice/righteousness (Rom. 3:25-26). It was where God justly and righteously punished sin. But even this is embedded in God's prior love. If he had not been pleased to set his love upon us, there would have been no cross, no atonement for sin, no sin-bearing sacrifice! Undeserved, gracious, sovereign love is the fountain-head of the gospel.

It is the love of God that sits underneath the momentous event of Calvary. Out of sight, like the great mass of an iceberg, it was God's love that both delivered Jesus up to the cross and supported him during his unimaginable agony on the cross. Octavius Winslow said it well: 'Who delivered up Jesus to die? Not Judas for money. Not the Jews for envy. Not Pilate for fear. But the Father for love.' John Owen understood this better than most:

> Eye the Father as love; look not on him as an always lowering [disapproving] father, but as one most kind and tender. Let us look on him by faith, as one that hath had thoughts of kindness towards us from everlasting.[1]

It would be a huge mistake to separate Jesus' life from his death on Calvary's cross. The cross was the climactic moment of Jesus' mission to seek and to save the lost. His cry 'It is finished' signalled the perfect fulfilling of his saving, substitutionary, atoning sacrifice. But the New Testament never separates Jesus' life from his death. Indeed, his whole life from his conception in Mary's womb till his death on the cross is considered 'one act of righteousness'

[1] John Owen, *Works* (London: Banner of Truth Trust, 1966), II:32.

by the apostle Paul (Rom. 5:18). We are never to conceive of Jesus' life merely as a means to an end: that is, he had to live in order to die. His life was as essential to our salvation as his death on the cross.

When Adam and Eve rebelled against God, disobeying his word to them (Gen. 2:17; 3:1-7), they brought God's just judgment and condemnation on the whole human race (Rom. 5:12-19). Adam was the appointed head of humanity; when he sinned, we all sinned 'in him', because we were united to him. We are all born into this world under God's just judgment. To be free from that just judgment we need to do two things: first, pay the penalty of our sin against God; second, live the perfect life that God requires of us. We are powerless and helpless to do either of these. But God found a way in his own Son to pay the penalty our sin deserved and to provide us with a perfect righteousness to enable us to be fit for fellowship in his presence. So, Jesus came to die the death our sins deserved and to provide us with the righteousness we all lack.

When the New Testament comes to explain the work of God's Son in our flesh, its most comprehensive way is to speak of Christ's 'obedience'. Jesus told his disciples that he had come from heaven not to do his own will but the will of the Father who sent him (John 6:38). Paul develops this note when he writes of Jesus, who was 'in the form of God', humbling himself and 'becoming obedient to the point of death, even death on a cross' (Phil. 2:6-8).

There is, of course, great significance in this idea that Jesus' whole life was a life of obedience to his heavenly

Father. In 1 Corinthians 15 Paul describes Jesus as 'the last Adam' and 'the second man' (1 Cor. 15:45-47). Adam's failure in the Garden of Eden was twofold: he departed from the way of obedience to God and his word; and secondly, his departure from the way of obedience was not at root a failure in obedience, but a failure in love. Adam was God's servant, but he was also God's 'son' (Luke 3:38). With all his privileges, Adam failed and brought the whole of humanity crashing down with him.

In his cross Jesus was no reluctant sin-offering: 'For this reason the Father loves me, because I lay down my life that I may take it up again. No one takes it from me, but I lay it down of my own accord' (John 10:17-18).

We have seen that in eternity, God's Son pledged himself to fulfil his Father's will and to do all that was necessary to save a people to God's praise and glory. Now that pledge has brought him to the cross. Of all the texts in the Gospel accounts of Jesus' passion, one in particular leads us into the cost to God of loving and saving a world of lost, judgment-deserving sinners, Matthew 27:46: 'And about the ninth hour Jesus cried out with a loud voice, saying, "Eli, Eli lema sabachthani?" that is, "My God, my God, why have you forsaken me?"'

Jesus has been on the cross for three pain-wracked hours. His whole body must have been crying out for relief, any kind of relief. His agony was unimaginable. Matthew tells us that 'there was darkness over all the land' (Matt. 27:45). Midday had become midnight. There is little doubt that the all-pervasive darkness was symbolic or sacramental of the all-consuming darkness that had engulfed Jesus' human soul. The undiluted wrath of God on sin had fallen in all its unrelieved intensity and justice on the great Sin-bearer (2 Cor. 5:21). In this moment of utter horror and darkness, the words of Psalm 22:1 explode from Jesus' lips ('with a loud voice'). But heaven is silent. No angel is sent now to help him, unlike a little earlier in the garden (Luke 22:43). No voice from heaven is heard to say, 'This is my beloved Son' as at his baptism and transfiguration (Matt. 3:17; 17:5). For Jesus all the lights have gone out. Darkness once again covers creation. And more, it covers creation's Creator.

But what did it mean for Jesus to be 'forsaken' by his Father?

We first need to say what it did not mean. It didn't mean, and couldn't mean, that there was a rupture in the Holy Trinity. God is eternally and perfectly and blessedly one in his tri-unity. Nor did it mean that Jesus only 'felt' he was forsaken. He does not ask why he feels forsaken, but why he *is* forsaken. The Son of God united to our flesh was forsaken, truly and really, by his Father. The cross is not an illusion, a charade, a sleight of hand. So, what did it mean for Jesus to be forsaken? There are depths we cannot begin to plumb. Here we are out of our depth. We have to say with Paul, 'Oh, the depth of the riches and wisdom and knowledge of God! How unsearchable are his judgments and how inscrutable his ways!' (Rom. 11:33). But while we cannot plumb the depths, we can dip our feet into them.

First, Jesus' cry was a cry of sinless perfection. He is where he is, not because he was personally deserving of this death, or of any death. He was God's own Son, his holy, sinless, faithfully obedient Son. In our frail flesh, he is experiencing not simply the physical agony of the cross; he is experiencing the agony of personal abandonment by his Father. Jesus' humanity was a true humanity, not a cloak to put on and then take off. He 'became flesh' (John 1:14).

Twice in his earthly ministry the Father had split the heavens to testify to his pleasure and pride in his Son. When Jesus was baptized at the commencement of his public ministry, the heavens were opened, the Spirit of God descended like a dove and rested on Jesus, and a voice from heaven said, 'This is my beloved Son, with whom I am well pleased' (Matt. 3:16-17). As Jesus neared Jerusalem where he would offer himself as a sacrifice for sin, he led Peter, James and John up a high mountain where he was 'transfigured before them' (Matt. 17:1-2). Again a voice from the glory cloud of God's presence said, 'This is my beloved Son, with whom I am well pleased; listen to him' (Matt. 17:5).

But now as Jesus hangs on the cross there is no voice from heaven. All is silent. The sinless Son of God is completely alone. Is it any wonder he cried, 'My God, my God, why have you forsaken me?' (Matt. 27:46).

Second, it was a cry of sin-bearing substitution. Jesus is enduring in the place of sinners what their sin against God deserved. He is experiencing in our place the hell our sin merited. Few men have more penetrated to the heart of this momentous cry than John 'Rabbi' Duncan: 'Forsaken by God—do you know what it was? It was damnation and damnation taken lovingly'. On the cross, God was executing in the person of his own Son the righteous wrath and judgment that sinners justly deserved. We can only begin to gauge the wickedness and horror of sin by seeing its condemnation in the bloodied, pain-wracked, abandoned person of the God-Man.

Jesus is on the cross as the sacrificial Lamb of God. He is the loving and just God's provision for our sin. He is dying, 'the righteous for the unrighteous, that he might bring us to God' (1 Pet. 3:18).

Third, it was a cry of bruised but unbowed faith and trust. Even in the extremity of his suffering Jesus cried, '*My* God, *my* God'. He has no longer any sense of the Father as Father. All he can say is, 'My God, my God, why?' This is the only occasion, even on the cross, when Jesus does not call God his Father. He did so in the agony of Gethsemane (Matt. 26:39). On the cross he prayed, 'Father, forgive them' (Luke 23:34). But now all he can say is, 'My *God*, my *God*'. But, while all the lights have gone out, his trust in God has not died. He is the perfect example of the man who fears the Lord: 'Who among you fears the LORD and obeys the voice of his servant? Let him who walks in darkness and has no light trust in the name of the LORD and rely on his God' (Isa. 50:10). Faith burned bright in a soul consumed with the darkness of divine wrath.

Fourth, it was the cry of a man upheld by the promised Holy Spirit. God had promised that he would put his Spirit on his Servant (Isa. 42:1). To Jesus the Holy Spirit was given without measure (John 3:34). As he hung on the cross, Jesus was being upheld moment by moment by the eternal Spirit

(Heb. 9:14). It is imperative we understand this. The cross was the concerted, agreed work of the Holy Trinity. Jesus is where he is as the sent one of the Father. It was the Father's love for the world that caused him not to spare his own Son but to give him up for us all (Rom. 8:32). Can it be doubted that even as the Father was pouring out his just wrath on his Son, in our place as our appointed covenant head, he was saying, 'If ever I loved you, my Jesus, 'tis now'?

It is in Jesus' cry, more than anywhere else, that we are given to see the sinfulness of sin. What must sin be if it took the God-forsakenness of God's own Son to atone for it? It is only really here that we come to have any sense of the sheer awfulness of sin. Our great problem is that we think of sin too horizontally: the mess it makes of ourselves and others (though that should not be ignored). But the real horror of sin is that it is rebellion against our Maker; it is a despising of his love, a defiance of his commandments, a repudiation of Jesus and his cross (Psa. 51:4). When you are next tempted to sin, little or large, think on this: 'If I yield to this temptation, I am despising God's love, defiantly trampling on his commandments, and repudiating Jesus and his cross, mocking his forsakenness.'

When I was a young lad, my desire not to hurt my mother was often enough to deter me from certain actions and words (God uses common graces as protectors). How much more should our desire not to grieve, offend, or bring dishonour to our Saviour keep us from yielding to temptation!

6

Salvation:
Union with Christ

In the New Testament Christians, perhaps surprisingly, are rarely called by that name. Only in Acts 11:26; 26:28; and 1 Peter 4:16 are believers in Jesus called 'Christians', 'Christ's ones'. The normal and almost invariable way they are described in the New Testament is as those who are 'in Christ'. This two-word description identifies the essential heart of what it means to be a Christian. A Christian is someone who has been brought, by God's grace, through faith, into a living, vital relationship with Jesus Christ. So much so, that he or she is 'in Christ', united indissolubly to him.

The New Testament pictures this union in a number of vivid metaphors. In 1 Corinthians 12:12-27, Christ is pictured as the head of the church and believers as his body (see also Rom. 12:4-5; Eph. 4:15-16). In John 15:1-17, Jesus describes his relationship to his disciples as that of a vine to its branches. In Ephesians 5:25-33, Paul likens Christ's relationship with his church to that of a husband with his wife (see also Rev. 21:2). In 1 Peter 2:4-8, the intimate relationship of believers to Christ is likened to that of 'living stones' joined together in a 'spiritual house' and connected to Christ the 'cornerstone'.

Union with Christ is the foundational truth in the Bible's teaching on salvation. John Murray wrote, 'Union with Christ is really the central truth of the whole doctrine of salvation.'[1] There are a number of things the New Testament impresses on us regarding the believer's union with Christ.

First, the Christian believer's union with Christ has its origin, not in the believer's choice of Christ, but in God's choice of the believer. God chose us 'in him [Christ] before the foundation of the world' (Eph. 1:4). Christian salvation has an eternal dimension and that eternal dimension is found in Christ. God's choosing of sinners to be saved and to be 'his own possession' (1 Pet. 2:9) is not the result ultimately of them choosing Christ, but the result of God choosing them 'in him before the foundation of the world'.

It is a remarkable and wonderful truth that the 'fountain of salvation'[2] is found in God the Father's eternal election of sinners 'in Christ' (Eph. 1:4). In this truth lies the Christian's great and invulnerable security. Our standing before God rests ultimately in his eternal choosing of us, not in our choosing of him.

---

[1] John Murray, *Redemption Accomplished and Applied*, (Edinburgh: Banner of Truth Trust, 2016), p. 165.

[2] *Ibid.*, p. 166.

In no sense, however, does God's eternal election of sinners in Christ undermine or nullify their decision to choose Christ. The gospel summons everyone, everywhere, to believe on the Lord Jesus Christ for salvation (Acts 16:30-31; 17:30; Eph. 2:8). We may not be able to understand how God's election of sinners in Christ 'fits' with our responsibility to believe the gospel. God does not ask us to understand how his sovereignty and our responsibility fit together. However, he does ask us to believe that they do.

Throughout the history of the church there have been Christians who have struggled to accept the Bible's teaching on God's sovereign election of sinners in Christ to salvation. But the teaching of the Bible could not be clearer. Jesus told his disciples, 'You did not choose me, but I chose you' (John 15:16). The apostle Peter addressed his first letter to the 'elect exiles of the Dispersion' (1 Pet. 1:1), and told them, 'you are a chosen race' (1 Pet. 2:9). The apostle Paul assured the Christians in Thessalonica that God had chosen them to be saved (2 Thess. 2:13). And as we have already noted, Paul blessed God the Father because he 'chose us in him [Christ] before the foundation of the world' (Eph. 1:4).

What we need to understand is that God's election of sinners in Christ is neither arbitrary nor unfair. All that God does he does wisely, never arbitrarily. And there is no unfairness in God. That God chooses to save anyone is a great wonder and mercy. God is obligated to save no one: 'for all have sinned and fall short of the glory of God' (Rom. 3:23). This is why one of the first responses of a forgiven sinner is to praise and thank God for his undeserved kindness and mercy. God's election does not breed pride, it provokes unbounded praise and wonder. We see this most magnificently in Romans 11:33-36, where Paul concludes his exposition of the sovereign, electing mercy of God in the gospel with a soaring doxology:

> Oh, the depth of the riches and wisdom and knowledge of God! How unsearchable are his judgments and how inscrutable his ways!
>> 'For who has known the mind of the Lord,
>> or who has been his counsellor?'
>> 'Or who has given a gift to him
>> that he might be repaid?'
> For from him and through him and to him are all things.
> To him be glory forever. Amen.

Second, union with Christ means that everything Jesus did, believers did 'in him'. In the New Testament Jesus is presented to us as a 'covenant or federal head'. Writing to the church in Corinth, Paul said, 'For as by a man came death, by a man has come also the resurrection of the dead. For as in Adam all die, so also in Christ shall all be made alive' (1 Cor. 15:21-22). Similarly, he writes to the Christians in Rome:

> as one trespass led to condemnation for all men, so one act of righteousness leads to justification and life for all men. For as by the one man's disobedience the many were made sinners, so by the one man's obedience the many will be made righteous (Rom. 5:18-19).

44

Do you see how Paul is presenting Adam and Christ as two representative heads? What one does, all who are united to him do. The one represents the many.

The Lord Jesus Christ did not come into the world as a private individual, but as the appointed covenant, representative head of all those given to him by his Father in eternity (John 6:38-40; 17:2). It is the Christian's union with Christ, the God-appointed covenant head of his people, that enables Paul to write that when Christ died, believers died with him, and that when Christ rose, believers rose with him (Rom. 6:1-11; 1 Cor. 15:22; Col. 2:20–3:4).

The Christian believer's identity is wholly bound up with Christ's identity because they are 'in him'. As he is, so they are. Paul puts this dramatically in Ephesians 2:6, where he tells us that God has 'raised us up with him and seated us with him in the heavenly places in Christ Jesus'. Even now, all Christians are so united to Jesus Christ that they are with him where he presently is, in the midst of God's throne (Rev. 7:17). If you are a Christian, this is true of you.

Third, when God chose sinners in Christ to be saved, he no less chose them to bring forth good works. Jesus emphasizes this in his teaching in John 15. Because the branches (that is, believers) are united to the 'true vine' (that is, Christ, John 15:1), they must bring forth 'fruit'. So much is this true, that Jesus said that bearing 'fruit' is what 'proves' we truly are his disciples (John 15:8).

Jesus does not spell out in John 15:8 precisely what he means by *bearing fruit*. However, in the verses that follow, he highlights two unmistakable marks or evidences of fruit-bearing:

First, keeping his commandments (John 15:10). A fruit-bearing life, a life that draws its vitality from 'the true vine' (John 15:1), will be a commandment-keeping life. Why? Because Jesus' life was a commandment-keeping life (John 15:10b). God the Father's ultimate purpose is to conform all believers to the likeness of his Son, in order that he might be the firstborn among many brothers (Rom. 8:29). That 'likeness' is a life shaped and styled by God's commands. The fruit that Jesus looks to see in our lives, the fruit that will *prove* we truly are his disciples, is a life that sweetly and lovingly seeks to obey everything that Jesus has commanded (Matt. 28:20). Notice the words 'sweetly and lovingly'. Jesus did not keep his Father's commands grudgingly or reluctantly. His obedience was the obedience of a loving Son. So with Christians. Our obedience is to be the overflow of lives that have been invaded by the grace and love of God in Christ.

Second, loving fellow Christians (John 15:12; 13:34-35). It is remarkable how emphatic the Bible is that our union with Christ will, of necessity, make itself known in the way we relate to, and treat, our fellow Christians. The apostle John had clearly taken Jesus' words to heart: 'By this all people will know that you are my disciples, if you have love for one another' (John 13:35). John also wrote in his first letter: 'We know that we have passed out of death into life, because we love the brothers' (1 John 3:14). A little later he makes the same point even more emphatically: 'If anyone says, "I love God", and hates his brother, he is a liar; for he who does not love his brother whom he has seen cannot love God whom he has not seen' (1 John 4:20).

This gives the lie to those who say that God's election in Christ of sinners to salvation can only breed pride and moral carelessness. On the contrary. Paul's response to people who were saying that the gospel he preached gave men and women the excuse to go on sinning is devastating:

> How can we who died to sin still live in it? Do you not know that all of us who have been baptized into Christ Jesus were baptized into his death? We were buried therefore with him by baptism into death, in order that, just as Christ was raised from the dead by the glory of the Father, we too might walk in newness of life (Rom. 6:2-4).

Continuing in sin is an impossibility for a Christian because we have been united to Jesus Christ in his death to sin and in his resurrection to a new life. Paul is not saying Christians do not sin. Sadly, tragically, we do. Rather he is making the same point the apostle John later makes: 'No one born of God makes a practice of sinning, for God's seed abides in him, and he cannot keep on sinning, because he has been born of God' (1 John 3:9).

God's wholly gracious choosing in Christ of sinners to be saved had from its inception a definite moral purpose. Having reminded the Ephesian Christians of God's sovereign and gracious election of them, Paul proceeded to impress on them that they were God's 'workmanship, created in Christ Jesus for good works, which God prepared beforehand, that we should walk in them' (Eph. 2:10). Good works are not in any sense the ground of the Christian's hope before God, but they are the inevitable fruit of any and every life united to Jesus Christ. James put the matter bluntly: 'faith by itself, if it does not have works, is dead' (James 2:17).

Fourth, the biblical truth of union with Christ is the greatest encouragement to believers. Union with Christ reminds us that all our hope and comfort before God lies outside of ourselves. John Owen understood this better than most (see the quotation on p. 34 above). Owen was deeply concerned that many Christians failed to grasp the grace of the Father's love in Christ:

> Unacquaintedness with our mercies and our privileges is our sin as well as our trouble. We harken not to the voice of the Spirit which is given unto us that we may know the things that are freely bestowed on us of God. This makes us go heavily when we might rejoice. And to be weak where we might be strong in the Lord. How few of the saints are experimentally acquainted with this privilege of holding immediate communion with the Father in love! With what anxious, doubtful thoughts do they look upon him! What fears, what questionings are there of his goodwill and kindness! At the best many think there is no sweetness at all in God towards us, but what is purchased at the high price of the blood of Jesus. It is true that that alone is the way of communication, but the free fountain and spring of all is in the bosom of the Father.[1]

[1] John Owen, *Works*, II:32.

Commenting on the Lord's words in Jeremiah 31:3 ('I have loved you with an everlasting love'), J. Geerhardus Vos wrote these words: 'The best proof that he will never cease to love us lies in that he never began.' I have never forgotten the effect these words had on me and continue to have on me. It is little wonder that C. H. Spurgeon wrote: 'Everlasting love shall be the pillow on which I rest my head tonight.'

7

Salvation's Great Accomplishment (1): God's Wrath Removed

In this chapter and the next, we will explore in a little more depth the Bible's teaching concerning the cross of Christ. We will especially ask the question, 'What did the cross of Christ achieve?'

When Jesus cried out in a loud voice from the cross, 'My God, my God, why have you forsaken me?', it must have seemed that the work entrusted to him by his Father was imperilled. But soon his cry of dereliction was followed by a cry of cosmic triumph, 'It is finished' (John 19:30).

What did Jesus mean when he cried, 'It is finished'?

What he certainly did not mean was that all his hopes were dying before his eyes. 'It is finished' was not a cry of resignation; it was a cry of triumph. Immediately he went on to say, '*Father*, into your hands I commit my spirit.' His sense of God being his Father had returned. The impenetrable darkness of his penal sufferings were over. The price had been paid. Victory was won.

'It is finished' meant that his obedience to the Father as his sin-bearing, sin-atoning Servant had come to its completion. He had been 'obedient to the point of death, even death on a cross' (Phil. 2:8). From the moment of his conception in the Virgin Mary's womb, Jesus had relentlessly, faithfully, and trustingly lived in obedience to his Father; even when the shadow of the cross penetrated his human soul in the garden, he said, 'not my will, but yours, be done' (Luke 22:42).

'It is finished' meant that the awful price of making atonement for sin had been paid in full. Jesus had drunk the cup filled to overflowing with God's righteous wrath against sin. What he had said in prayer to his Father, I [have] accomplished the work you gave me to do' (John 17:4), was now a fact. Nothing more was needed. All had been done. The work of atonement was finished. By one act of perfect obedience and sacrifice (Rom. 5:19), God in Christ provided pardon and peace for everyone who believes in Jesus.

But there was work to be done beyond the *tetelestai* (the one Greek word translated as 'It is finished'). Our Lord Jesus is not existing in self-indulgent ease in heaven's glory. He continues as our great high priest to intercede for us at God's right hand, blessing us and as our King preserving us from all his and our enemies (Heb. 7:25; John 17:2), giving eternal life to all those given to him by his Father.

The Bible has its own technical, theological language to help us grasp the saving significance of Jesus' 'It is finished'.

When I started secondary school I entered a new world of learning. Words I had never heard before were daily assaulting my ears: Gaelic words, long, multi-syllabic mathematical words, weird (as it seemed to me) chemical formulae. If I were going to make any progress in these subjects, I needed to learn the new vocabularies. The world of the Bible has a unique vocabulary and if you remain ignorant of the vocabulary, you will remain at best stunted in your Christian life, and at worst a spiritual pauper.

'Propitiation' is one of the Bible's 'big words', big not only in terms of its length, but more profoundly in terms of its significance. Propitiation sheds light on the heart and glory of the gospel of Christ. Perhaps it is a relatively unknown word to some, or even to many, reading these pages. But it is a word that needs to be understood because it wonderfully explains the significance and glory of the cross.

In Romans 3:25 Paul writes of Jesus Christ, 'whom God put forward as a propitiation by his blood'. We all know what it means to propitiate someone, even if we don't know the word itself. You propitiate someone when you appease them and turn away their hostility to you or disappointment with you. Perhaps you have failed and even hurt someone you love. You want to make amends. You want to put things right. You want your relationship with them restored and the anger or hurt removed. So, to make things right, to appease them, you might give them a gift, a token of your sorrow and love.

But why does God need to be propitiated? For many professional theologians and even, sadly, many professing

Christians, propitiation is a bad word. Why? For this reason: they say, 'God is love. God is kind. God is grieved by our sin, but he is not angered by it. Sin makes God sad, but it does not make him angry. God is not like the deities of the unenlightened heathens who must have sacrifices offered to them to win their favour. We need to be reconciled to God. But God does not need to be reconciled to us', so we are told by such people.

But we have a problem. The *Bible* tells us from beginning to end that God hates sin and is angry with sinners 'all the day long'. You may not like what the Bible says, but you cannot ignore what it says, or hide from what it says, or pretend it doesn't say what it says (Rom. 1:18; 2:5; Luke 12:4-5). God needs to be propitiated because he is who he is. Sin is an affront to God. Sin offends God. Sin is rebellion against God. Sin makes me and not God the centre of the universe.

Sin is the ultimate excluder. God cannot politely ignore our sin and refuse to be angry with us for one simple reason: *he is who he is*. Paul makes this point in Romans 3:25-26. He has just said that God put Christ forward as a 'propitiation by his blood' and this he did 'to show [his] righteousness'. To reinforce the point, Paul says it again: 'It was to show his righteousness at the present time' that God 'put forward' his own Son to make propitiation for our sins.

This leads us to ask the question, 'How can God be propitiated? How can God's righteous anger be turned away from me?' The Bible's answer is stunning: God himself provided the propitiation that would turn away his wrath and remove everything that separates him from us and us from him. God 'put forward' his incarnate Son 'as a propitiation by his blood' (Rom. 3:25).

God himself in his own Son became the propitiation. The phrase 'by his blood' is the Bible's shorthand for 'by his sin-bearing, sin-atoning, wrath-quenching offering on the cross'. To this all the Old Testament sacrifices pointed and signified.

'Propitiation presupposes the wrath and displeasure of God.'[1] This truth does not sit easily with many inside and outside the church today. But it is a truth to which the whole Bible testifies, a truth that impresses on us both the perfect holiness of God and the utter sinfulness of sin. What is completely missed, however, in those who object to the idea that God needs to be propitiated, is that the cross of Christ does not turn a wrathful God into a loving God. Rather, it is God's own love for the world that causes him to provide a propitiation for the sins of the world (1 John 2:2), and the propitiation is his own Son, the Lord Jesus Christ. The apostle John understood exactly this great truth: 'In this is love, not that we have loved God but that he loved us and sent his Son to be the propitiation for our sins' (1 John 4:10). What a God! What a gospel!

[1] John Murray, *Redemption Accomplished and Applied*, p. 24.

8

Salvation's Great Accomplishment (2): Redemption in Christ

'Redemption' is another of the great words in the Bible. To understand its significance we need to appreciate its Old Testament roots. In the Old Testament, the great act of redemption was God's deliverance of Israel from its slavery in Egypt. Redemption, however, means more than deliverance. It means deliverance through costly effort. Redemption is costly. This point is made in Exodus 13:14: 'By a strong hand the LORD brought us out of Egypt, from the house of slavery.' Rescuing his people from their bondage was not an effortless act on God's part. It was by 'a strong hand', that is, by the exertion of his almighty power, God rescued his people from their captivity in Egypt.

Why we need redemption

But the great captivity that enslaves God's people is not captivity to any mere earthly power. Jesus said, 'Truly, truly, I say to you, everyone who practices sin is a slave to sin' (John 8:34). Paul tells the Christians in Rome that they 'were once slaves of sin' (Rom. 6:17). The sad and tragic state of every human being is that we follow the prince of the power of the air and are by nature children of God's wrath (Eph. 2:2-3). Sin is not an occasional, troublesome intruder, it is an enslaving power. And we are powerless in and of ourselves to do anything about this bondage to sin and its master Satan. This is why we need redemption. We need to be rescued from this sorry servitude and set free to become 'slaves of righteousness' (Rom. 6:18). This is what the Lord Jesus Christ has done for us: 'In him we have redemption through his blood, the forgiveness of our trespasses' (Eph. 1:7). Redemption from the guilt and domineering power of sin and Satan is one of the glorious blessings of our union with Christ.

The question arises: But how does the blood of Christ bring about our redemption from sin and Satan? Again we need to go back to the Old Testament fully to appreciate the connection between 'blood' and 'redemption'.

In the rich symbolism and typology of the Old Testament sacrificial system, God's holy wrath and just judgment were turned aside by the offering up of a spotless sacrifice in the place of the sinner. The letter to the Hebrews wonderfully captures the heart of the Old Testament sacrificial system and explains its significance:

> But when Christ appeared as a high priest of the good
> things that have come … he entered once for all into the
> holy places, not by means of the blood of goats and calves

but by means of his own blood, thus securing an eternal redemption (Heb. 9:11-12).

Jesus paid in full the price of our redemption. He offered himself, in our place, as our substitute, to pay the ransom price that we could never pay—the price of removing the sin that enslaved us to Satan.

Our sins had made a separation between us and God (Isa. 59:2). If we were ever to be rescued from our enslaved and hell-bound state, we needed God to step in and do for us what we were powerless to do for ourselves: remove the sin that separated him from us and made us Satan's captives. This he has done, unimaginably and unfathomably in his Son, Jesus Christ.

God is holy and could never simply wave a wand and make our sin disappear. But in his glorious grace, and in his beloved Son, God has found a way righteously and holily to punish our sin and to rescue us from our abysmal captivity to sin and Satan.

It is imperative that we rightly understand what Paul is telling us. He is not saying that a gracious, love-filled Son persuaded his wrath-filled Father to redeem us through his sin-bearing death on the cross. The Son of God is always the sent one of his Father. It was the love of the heavenly Father that set forth Jesus 'as a propitiation by his blood, to be received by faith' (Rom. 3:25).

Nor is there anything unbecoming or inappropriate in the Lord Jesus Christ taking our place on the cross. From the moment of his conception in the womb of the Virgin

Mary, through the overshadowing power of the Holy Spirit, God's Son in our flesh was living and breathing and acting not for himself, but for us. All that Jesus did, he did, not for himself but for all those he represented before God. Just as we fell in Adam our first head, so we are raised in Christ our second and last head (see Rom. 5:12-21; 1 Cor. 15:21-23, 47-49).

Jesus' death on the cross was a death of infinite significance and of infinite effectiveness. He was the spotless Lamb of God on whom the Father laid all our sin and shame (Isa. 53:6, 10). In his own blood he paid the price of our sin.

By his representative, substitutionary blood-shedding on Calvary, God's Son, in our flesh, won for us the forgiveness of our 'trespasses'. The righteous judgment and condemnation our sin against God deserved was executed on God's own Son, the representative God-Man.

It is little wonder that, once again, Paul tells us that God did this for us 'according to the riches of his grace' (Eph. 1:7). He never tires of reminding us that everything we now posses in Christ is the result and fruit of the riches of God's grace. Salvation is of the Lord. 'Not to us, O LORD, not to us, but to your name give glory, for the sake of your steadfast love and your faithfulness!' (Psa. 115:1).

Jesus Christ is our covenant head, the one appointed in eternity by God to be the Redeemer of God's elect. God, in his own Son, executed the unimaginable judgment that our sin deserved. 'For our sake he made him to be sin who knew no sin, so that in him we might become the righteousness

of God' (2 Cor. 5:21). This was Jesus' self-conscious understanding of his mission: 'For even the Son of Man came not
to be served but to serve, and to give his life as a ransom
for many' (Mark 10:45).

The blessing of redemption

The first benefit flowing to us from Christ's redemption is
'the forgiveness of our trespasses'. To be a forgiven sinner,
to know that God is no longer against you but for you in
Christ, is truly liberating. If Christ has atoned for us in our
sin and rebellion, and in his own blood-shedding paid the
price of our sin, then we are free, free to live unto God as
his now forgiven, adopted sons. Do we sufficiently marvel
at the forgiveness of sins? In Christ, God has blotted out
all our sins (Acts 3:19) and removed them from us 'as far
as the east is from the west' (Psa. 103:12). 'In him we have
redemption' (Eph. 1:7). Redemption in Christ is a settled
fact, an unchangeable, never-to-be-altered, fact.

'You are not your own'

Christ's redemption of sinners by his blood-shedding has
an immediate implication for, and application to, sinners.
His redemption means that we are not our own, for we have
been bought with a price. 'So,' Paul tells the Corinthians,
'glorify God in your body' (1 Cor. 6:20). It is one thing to
confess the truth of the blood redemption of Christ and
another to live as a blood-redeemed, forgiven sinner, glori-
fying God concretely in our bodies. Let us then bring into
captivity every thought to the obedience of Christ (2 Cor.

10:5) and present our bodies to God as living sacrifices, which is our spiritual worship (Rom. 12:1).

And, not surprisingly, Paul once again tells us that this redemption in Christ is 'according to the riches of his grace'. Paul never wearies of magnifying the God of grace. He wants us never to forget for a moment that we are, and ever will be, 'debtors to mercy alone'. The grace of God is more than a theological or denominational distinctive. The mark of a man or woman captured and captivated by grace is a humble and worship-filled life. Doxology is the great goal of biblical, authentic Christian faith. If it is not, then grace, gospel grace, is absent.

9

The Grace of Salvation:
God's Electing Love

For many people the doctrines of God's sovereign election of sinners to eternal life and God's love are mutually exclusive. Election is conceived as arbitrary, if not cold and clinical, while love is conceived as God's ultimate resolve, in his kind mercy, to embrace everyone, everywhere, in every age. How is it possible that such a God, who is love (1 John 4:8), could conceivably choose some sinners to eternal life while passing by other sinners, condemning them to eternal and unremitting misery? Would this not, by definition, make God arbitrary and selective? Would it not expose his claim to be all-loving as a pious fraud?

Robert Burns famously parodied the doctrine of election in 'Holy Willie's Prayer' (1785). The poem, which records the (fictional) self-justifying prayer of a church elder, Holy Willie, is an attack on the bigotry and hypocrisy of the Scottish Kirk. Throughout the poem, Holy Willie's hypocrisy is exposed as he asks God to judge harshly and show no mercy to his fellow transgressors. Burns used the example of Holy Willie to make the point that the Calvinist theology underpinning the entire Kirk was equally hypocritical:

> O Thou, that in the heavens does dwell,
> Wha, as it pleases best Thysel',
> Sends ane to heaven an' ten to hell,
>   A' for Thy glory,
> And no for ony guid or ill
>   They've done before Thee.

Does this arbitrary and clinical attitude remotely reflect the biblical teaching on election?

The first thing we must do is to discover what the Bible has to say in this matter. This is critical and crucial. If our starting point is what the fallen and sinful mind of man can conceive, then we are bound to construct a theology that fallen, sinful man can make sense of. But the true starting point of theology is not the musings of mere fallen men, but the revelation of the living God.

It is a great sadness that the doctrine of election should have been such a source of controversy within the Christian church. Remarkably, the apostle Paul was neither puzzled nor embarrassed by this doctrine. On the contrary, he embraced it, and even gloried in the grace and wonder of it:

> Blessed be the God and Father of our Lord Jesus Christ … even as he chose us in him before the foundation of the world, that we should be holy … In love he predestined us for adoption … to the praise of his glorious grace (Eph. 1:3-6).

When John Calvin began to expound the doctrine of election ('Eternal election, by which God has predestined some to salvation, others to destruction'), he issued a warning:

> Human curiosity renders the discussion of predestination, already somewhat difficult of itself, very confusing and even dangerous. No restraints can hold it back from wandering in forbidden bypaths … If allowed, it will leave no secret to God that it will not search out and unravel … First, then, let them remember that when they inquire into predestination they are penetrating the sacred precincts of divine wisdom. If anyone with carefree assurance breaks into this place, he will not succeed in satisfying his curiosity and he will enter a labyrinth from which he can find no exit.[1]

Calvin's warning is ever timely. We must approach the revelation of God's truth with humble, reverent and attentive minds and hearts. We must be prepared to be astonished, humbled, and even perplexed, for 'Who has known the mind of the Lord?' (Rom. 11:34). Certainly not sinful, fallible men and women!

Throughout the Bible God's sovereign choice of sinners for a preordained destiny is presented as an act of grace. Grace is undeserved kindness to judgment-deserving sinners. Thomas Goodwin memorably described what grace is:

> Grace is more than mercy and love, it superadds to them. It denotes not simply love, but the love of a sovereign,

---

[1] John Calvin, *Institutes*, III.xx.1.

transcendly [*sic*] superior, one that may do what he will, that may wholly choose whether he will love or no … Now God, who is an infinite Sovereign, who might have chosen whether ever he would love us or no, for him to love us, this is grace.

If there is any one truth that the New Testament, or for that matter the whole Bible, wants to highlight, emphasize, and indelibly impress upon us, it is that God's salvation in Jesus Christ cannot be earned, deserved, or in any way merited. Salvation is wholly and completely and absolutely 'of the Lord'. We have seen how Paul has stressed this in the centrality he gives to 'faith' as the only means by which we are justified before God. There is no merit in faith. Indeed the very opposite. Faith is trust in another; faith is the acknowledgement that all our hope lies outside of ourselves. The old hymn 'Rock of Ages' captures the truth:

> Nothing in my hand I bring,
> Simply to Thy cross I cling:
> Naked, come to Thee for dress;
> Helpless, look to Thee for grace;
> Foul, I to the fountain fly:
> Wash me, Saviour, or I die![1]

This is such an important matter for Paul that he tells us twice over in Romans 3:24 that God's justification of sinners has nothing whatsoever to do with anything in them, or done by them: we 'are justified by his grace as a gift'.

---

[1] The well-known hymn was written by Augustus M. Toplady (1740–78)

Before we reflect on these words, ask yourself this question: Why is Paul, and why is the Bible, so determined to impress this truth on us? The answer is obvious, is it not? Faith kills boasting (Rom. 3:27). It is Paul's jealous concern for God's glory that makes him so repetitive. We have nothing to boast about before God, and we need to know that, believe that, and live in the controlling and liberating power of that truth. The first and greatest issue of the gospel is not that sinners are justified by faith alone, but that salvation is by God's grace alone.

First, Paul says that God justifies sinners as a 'gift', that is, *freely*, without any cost whatsoever (Rom. 3:24). This is wonderfully good news because we have nothing to give to God. We have nothing which deserves in any way acceptance with God. God justifies sinners as the gift of his grace, a gift with no strings attached, a gift of his love in Christ. And in the gospel God offers and holds out this free gift to everyone everywhere. More than that, he personally pleads with us all to receive his gift (2 Cor. 5:20; Isa. 55:1). All you and I can do is receive this gift; we can never earn it, buy it, or deserve it. If we could deserve it, it would no longer be a 'gift'; it would be a 'reward' (Rom. 4:4).

Second, God justifies sinners 'by his grace'. Paul cannot tell us too often that salvation is all of God. *Grace* is probably the most used and least understood and appreciated word in the vocabulary of the Christian church. If you look at any Roman Catholic catechism or handbook on doctrine, the word *grace* appears everywhere. But if you were to ask, 'Please spell "grace"', it would most likely be spelled '*works*'. But grace is God's undeserved kindness and mercy to judgment-deserving sinners.

We must pause and understand something profound about grace. Grace is not a blessing that God scoops out of his heavenly treasury to pour down on judgment-deserving sinners. God's grace is inextricably tied to Jesus Christ. Jesus *himself* is the grace of God (2 Cor. 8:9). When Paul tells us that we 'are justified by his grace as a gift', he means, as the whole passage tells us, that we are justified in and by Jesus Christ. It is Christ's 'blood' (Rom. 5:9), his sin-atoning sacrifice on the cross, that justifies us. He is the one who is 'full of grace' (John 1:14).

This is not merely a matter of theology. God's salvation is not 'a thing' he gives to us, not even a blessed 'thing'. Jesus himself is the salvation of God. When old Simeon held the infant Jesus in his arms in the temple, he said, 'Lord, now you are letting your servant depart in peace, according to your word; for my eyes have seen your salvation' (Luke 2:27-30). He understood that salvation was not a *something* but a *someone*.

We must now pause and ask ourselves another question: If God's justification is wholly a gift of his grace, and I profess to believe that, how then will it show itself in my life? What does a sovereign-grace-confessing life look like?

First, it will, above all, be a doxological life, a life that overflows with wonder, love and praise (cf. Rom. 11:33-36). It will not be hard-nosed and hard-edged. It will not be smug. It will be a praise-filled life and not an argumentative life.

Second, it will be a sacrificially-obedient life: 'I appeal to you therefore, brothers, by the mercies of God, to present your bodies as a living sacrifice, holy and acceptable to God, which is your spiritual worship' (Rom. 12:1). Notice the word 'therefore'. As Paul looks back on his exposition of the gospel of God's grace in Christ, he tells us that our response to 'the mercies of God' must be one of unconditional giving of all that we are to the God who gave his Son for us. Unconditionalism should be a distinguishing mark of every Christian. With Isaiah we should always be saying, 'Here I am! Send me' (Isa. 6:8).

Third, it will be a church-committed life. God's grace in Christ not only unites us to his Son, it unites us in him to all other believers. The life of faith cannot be lived atomistically or individualistically. It can only be lived in fellowship, in connectedness with other believers (read 1 Cor. 12:12-27). The purpose of the gospel is not to save multitudes of people and then leave them to live any which way they think best. God gives his sheep pastors and teachers and elders to shepherd and feed them, to help mould them into a family, a bride fit for the Lord Jesus Christ (Eph. 4:11-16).

In other words, God chooses to save sinners not because of anything in them, because there is nothing in them worthy of his blessing. He chooses to save sinners because it has pleased him to set his love upon them.

However, if we are to make any sense of this we must take a step back and consider what God's word teaches us about ourselves.

The proper (that is biblical) starting point for our thinking about election must be the fallenness of the whole human race in Adam. 'None is righteous, no, not one … all have sinned and fall short of the glory of God' (Rom. 3:10, 23). Paul goes on in Romans 5:12 to explain the source of this tragedy: 'sin came into the world through one man, and death through sin, and so death spread to all men because all sinned'. Our union with Adam in his sin, and the corruption of our natures through his sin and our own sin, has brought us all under God's just and holy condemnation. We are all 'by nature children of [God's] wrath' (Eph. 2:3). Not one child of Adam who has ever lived has any claim upon God. The wonder of the gospel is not that God chooses to save some, but that God has been pleased to save any!

God's choice is not in any sense occasioned by meritorious achievements on the part of those he chooses. Election is all of grace and grace excludes merit absolutely. Paul makes the point unequivocally in Romans 11:5-6: 'So too at the present time there is a remnant, chosen by grace. But if it is by grace, it is no longer on the basis of works; otherwise grace would no longer be grace.'

God's gracious election is, then, free and unconditional. God owes us nothing, except his righteous condemnation. If God is pleased to choose anyone to be saved, how can he be charged with injustice of any kind? The Lord himself said to Moses, 'I will have mercy on whom I have mercy, and I will have compassion on whom I have compassion' (Rom. 9:15). 'So then,' Paul continues, 'it depends not on human will or exertion, but on God, who has mercy' (Rom. 9:16).

All this, of course, is repugnant to the world we live in. Men and women have a high sense of their own importance and a low sense of God's greatness and glory. Sin, if it exists at all, is a minor blemish, a little local difficulty, not the heinous crime the Bible makes it out to be. God, if he exists at all, is conceived of as having an obligation to do us good, to wink at our rebellion against him, and to move heaven and earth to pander to our needs (even to our whims). This is simply an expression of the twistedness of our fallen, sinful nature. Sin shows itself in our thinking too much of ourselves and too little of our Creator. George Swinnock, a contemporary of Goodwin's, could have been speaking of our own day when he wrote:

> We take the size of sin too low, and short, and wrong, when we measure it by the wrong it doth to ourselves, or our families, or our neighbours, or the nation wherein we live; indeed, herein somewhat of its evil and mischief doth appear; but to take its full length and proportion, we must consider the wrong it doth to this great, this glorious, this incomparable God. Sin is incomparably malignant, because the God principally injured by it is incomparably excellent.[1]

Until this fact dawns upon us, the doctrine of God's gracious election will always be anathema to us. But when the true seriousness and wickedness of sin overwhelms our proud hearts, then we will marvel at the wonder that God should ever have been pleased to save one sinner, far less a multitude which no man can number.

[1] George Swinnock, *Works* (Edinburgh: Banner of Truth Trust, 1992), IV:456.

10

Receiving Salvation:
By Faith Alone

If a survey was undertaken to discover what has been the greatest discovery in the past 500 years, I wonder what would top the poll. I especially wonder if anyone would agree with me that the greatest discovery was made by a German Augustinian monk by the name of Martin Luther around the year 1515. What did Luther discover? Simply this: he discovered that, in the gospel of Jesus Christ, the righteousness of God was not a crushing revelation but a saving revelation, a revelation of his way of bringing sinners righteously into an eternally right relationship with himself. The gospel really was *good* news (Rom. 1:16-17).

This truth had been buried under an avalanche of church traditions for centuries. The church said, 'Do your best, try your hardest, do your penances, trust the church, and it may go well with you.' Luther discovered that the Bible said something very different: 'Your best will never be good enough, no matter how hard you try; so trust in Christ alone and it certainly will go well with you'. This discovery transformed Europe, and beyond Europe, the whole world.

In Romans 3:19-20 Paul leaves us asking, 'Is that it? Am I without any hope?' No, hope abounds because 'the righteousness of God has been manifested apart from the law, although the Law and the Prophets bear witness to it' (Rom. 3:21). In Jesus Christ, the righteous God has found a way to justify, to declare righteous, and then to make righteous, unrighteous sinners. Think through with me Paul's densely compacted argument.

First, God has 'manifested' or 'revealed' his righteousness, his way of justifying sinners. He has not kept it hidden; he has made it known, plainly, clearly, gloriously. God has not revealed his way of salvation to an elite few: we are not dependent on the authority of the church or the intellect of the academy to make known to us 'the righteousness of God', his way of making sinners right with himself. God himself has revealed clearly and plainly his way of salvation in his Son, Jesus Christ.

Second, God's saving righteousness is 'apart from law' (notice that in the original Greek there is no definite article, 'the', before 'law'). Paul could be thinking about the fatal flaw in Judaism: that if I do my best and try my hardest, in the end all will be will with me. Or he could be thinking more universally: at the heart of every man and woman everywhere is the thought, 'If I do my best, God will accept me.' But Paul has exploded the falseness and absurdity of that thought in Romans 1:18–3:20. This holds true for those of us who profess to be Christians. We can only too easily slip into a way of thinking that says, 'God will accept me because I am Reformed, read my Bible, say my prayers, have grown in holiness.' But God justifies no one on the basis of law, no one (Rom. 3:22, 25, 26).

Third, Paul immediately balances what he has just said: God's saving righteousness is witnessed to by 'the Law and the Prophets'. The last thing Paul wanted to do was give the impression that the old dispensation was bankrupt of gospel (3:31). In Romans 4, Paul illustrates from the lives of Abraham and David, two old-covenant men, the truth of God's saving righteousness. The whole Old Testament looked forward with increasing eagerness to the fulfilment in history of God's promised salvation (1 Pet. 1:10-12; John 8:56). Here we see so clearly the fundamental relationship between the Old and New Testaments, the relationship of promise to fulfilment, of type to antitype, of shadow to reality, of incomplete to complete, *not* of less true to more true.

Fourth, Paul now tells us that the saving righteousness of God is 'through faith … for all who believe' (see also Rom. 1:17). It is possible to translate, 'through the faithfulness or faith of Jesus Christ'. It is absolutely true that God's saving righteousness rests on the absolute faithfulness of Christ, faithfulness that took him to the sin-bearing death on the cross (Rom. 5:19; Phil. 2:8). But it is far more natural and contextual to follow the traditional translation. Why then does Paul add, 'for all who believe'? Is this not unnecessary repetition? It is repetition, but not unnecessary repetition. Paul has an excellent theological and evangelistic reason; he wants to highlight and underscore the universal availability of God's righteousness. God's saving righteousness is for everyone (Gentile as well as Jew) who believes.

Understanding faith

It has often been said that the natural default belief of the human heart is that God accepts sinners on the basis of their good works, whether accomplished or intended. The teaching of the Bible is that the only person God has accepted or will ever accept on the basis of good works is Jesus Christ (see Phil. 2:8-11; notice the 'Therefore' at the beginning of verse 9). The Bible is wholly unflattering when it comes to depict the human condition (Rom. 3:9ff.). The fundamental problem with people who think that their good works are good enough to bring them into the glory of God's eternal presence is … What would you say? That they have too high an estimate of themselves? True. But there is a more basic and fundamental flaw in their thinking: *they have too low an estimate of God*. They think God is simply a bigger, even grander version of themselves (Psa. 50:21).

Until you grasp this, you shut yourself out of God's salvation. Not one of us is good enough. There is, however, one who is good enough. Our great need therefore is to be vitally connected to him. This is what Paul is telling us again and again in these verses (Rom. 3.22, 25, 26, 28, 30; 4:5).

It would be a huge mistake, therefore, if you thought that Paul is telling us that 'faith' is what justifies us before God. The heart of the gospel is not '*Believe* on the Lord Jesus Christ and you will be saved', but 'Believe *on the Lord*

Jesus Christ and you will be saved.' It is not faith that saves you; it is the Lord Jesus Christ. Faith did not die for you as a sin-bearing, sin-atoning sacrifice. It was the Lord Jesus Christ who was made sin for us, so that in him we might become the righteousness of God (2 Cor. 5:21)! Never once does the New Testament tell us that sinners are justified before God on the ground of faith. God justifies believing sinners by Christ's blood (Rom. 5:9). Jesus Christ himself is our righteousness (1 Cor. 1:30). Faith is what takes us into Christ, in whom God 'justifies the ungodly' (Rom. 4:5). In Christ, God's own righteousness is counted ours, just as our sins were counted Christ's (2 Cor. 5:21; Phil. 3:9).

This needs to be said for a number of reasons, but perhaps, above all, for this reason: *the centre of the life of faith is not faith, but the Lord Jesus Christ.* The focus of the life of faith is not the quality of my faith, but the grace of the Lord Jesus Christ.

What then is the faith that brings us into saving union with Christ?

First, faith is self-renouncing trust in the Lord Jesus Christ. Saving faith contains knowledge and acknowledgment. But there is another, vital and necessary aspect to faith. Faith is our response to the awful discovery that 'in me there dwells no good thing', that my only hope before God lies outside of myself. Horatius Bonar (1808–89) said it well:

> Upon a life I did not live,
> Upon a death I did not die;

> Another's life, Another's death,
> I stake my whole eternity.[1]

Second, faith is directed solely and alone to the person and work of the Lord Jesus Christ. Faith says and sings,

> Other refuge have I none,
> Hangs my helpless soul on Thee.[2]

The object of faith is a person. Belief in the *Westminster Confession of Faith,* or some other great summary of the Bible's teaching, will not save you. No creed or confession, however excellent, can save anyone. No parents, however godly and Christlike, can save anyone. No church, however orthodox and faithful, can save anyone. Jesus Christ alone saves.

Faith is propositional. That is, it is fixed and focused on vital truths presented in the Bible. The Jesus we cast ourselves upon is the incarnate Son of God, the sin-bearing, sin-atoning, death-defeating, bodily risen, and reigning Lord. The Christian faith is natively doctrinal. But doctrines don't save; it is Jesus who saves. Jesus truly is a doctrinal Jesus. We must be careful, however, not to separate Jesus from the truths about him. John Calvin put this well when he spoke of Christ coming to us 'clothed with his gospel'.[3] Put bluntly, it is not believing that justification is by faith alone that will save you; it is believing that Jesus himself is your saving righteousness, that he is

---

[1] From his hymn 'On Merit Not My Own I Stand'.
[2] From the hymn 'Jesus, Lover of My Soul', by Charles Wesley (1707–88).
[3] John Calvin, *Institutes,* III.ii.6.

your salvation, that he brings you into an eternally right standing and relationship with God.

It is sometimes said that this teaching is simply theological sleight of hand. How can God justly punish someone who is righteous and somehow transfer the righteousness of that person to others who are guilty before God? All that God does, he does justly (Rom. 3:26). The answer to this objection lies in this: Jesus Christ is not a private man but a covenant head (Rom. 5:12-21; 1 Cor. 15:22). God's Son came into this dark world as the representative head of all his people. As Thomas Goodwin quaintly put it, all men and women are tied either to Christ's girdle strings or to Adam's. What Jesus did, he did not for himself but for all who would ever believe in him throughout the ages. His life is my life; his death is my death; his resurrection is my resurrection (Rom. 6:1-14). All he did, he did for me.

Third, faith is God-glorifying trust in the Lord Jesus Christ. God's proximate purpose in sending his Son into our world was to save a people from sin and death and hell and bring them to heaven as the bride of his Son. This was his proximate purpose. But God has a more ultimate purpose than this. His ultimate purpose concerns not the salvation of sinners but the exaltation of his Son, their Saviour (Rom. 8:29). Every exercise of faith brings glory to God and honour to the Lord Jesus Christ.

Fourth, faith is God's gift. Faith is not a dormant sixth sense we all possess, which is just waiting for us to spring it into action. Faith is the gift of God (Eph. 2:8). However, it is not God who believes for you. Faith is the individual coming to Jesus Christ and casting the whole weight of their confidence upon him, the crucified and risen Saviour. The focus in the New Testament is not on the *origin* of faith but on the *duty* of faith. God commands everyone everywhere to believe (Isa. 45:22; Acts 17:30-31, 34). Much more, God even pleads with everyone everywhere to believe on his Son (Ezek. 33:11; 2 Cor. 5:20).

In the gospel of his Son, God gives us what we do not have, what we could never provide for ourselves, and what we most desperately need. This is why the Christian never, ever, has any cause for boasting (Rom. 3:27-28). Christians are debtors to mercy alone. And so we say, 'Not to us, O LORD, not to us, but to your name give glory, for the sake of your steadfast [covenant] love and your faithfulness!' (Psa. 115:1).

11

Salvation's Highest Privilege: Adoption into God's Family

The New Testament confronts us with the staggering truth that God has not only chosen us in Christ to be saved and to be 'holy and blameless', he has also 'predestined us for adoption through Jesus Christ' (Eph. 1:5). God's salvation in Christ has a familial shape. Adoption has been called the apex or omega point of God's blessings to us in Christ. In our union with Adam our first head we fell into sin and became the children of God's wrath (Eph. 2:3). In union with Christ our second and ultimate head, we are brought into the consummate heights of sonship to God.

Jesus is the eternal Son of God in our flesh. Because of God's predestined purpose, 'through Jesus Christ', we have been 'adopted as sons' of the heavenly Father. Jesus has 'brothered' us in his gospel (Heb. 2:11). He has done this, first by becoming one with us in his incarnation (Heb. 2:11), and then, as our representative covenant head, dying in our place, bearing God's just condemnation on our sin, and rising for our justification (Rom. 4:25).

The grace of adoption

God's gracious adoption of sinners is a much-neglected truth. He chose us, saved us, and sanctified us in order to make us his adopted children. God is our Father in Christ. We are his sons and daughters, with all the privileges of sons and daughters. The *Westminster Confession of Faith* has a magnificent chapter on adoption:

> All those that are justified, God vouchsafeth, in and for his only Son Jesus Christ, to make partakers of the grace of adoption: by which they are taken into the number, and enjoy the liberties and privileges of the children of God; have his name put upon them; receive the Spirit of adoption; have access to the throne of grace with boldness; are enabled to cry, Abba, Father; are pitied, protected, provided for, and chastened, by him, as by a father; yet, never cast off, but sealed to the day of redemption, and inherit the promises, as heirs of everlasting salvation.[1]

Jesus and his disciples

As Jesus began his public ministry he sought to impress on his disciples that God was their Father. In the Sermon on the Mount (Matt. 5-7), Jesus often spoke to his disciples of their new relationship with God because of their belonging to him. In Matthew 6, Jesus spoke of God as his disciples' Father twelve times ('your Father', eight times; 'your heavenly Father', three times; 'our Father', once). In one chapter God is spoken of as his people's Father more times than in the whole of the Old Testament. This does not

---

[1] *Westminster Confession of Faith*, XII.1.

mean that God was more of a father to his new covenant people than he was to his old covenant people. It does mean that in Christ, God's familial relationship to his people has come out from the shadows into the noonday light of the incarnation of God's Son.

Jesus' teaching in Matthew 6 is as much pastoral as it is theological. He wants his disciples to know the grace and wonder of their familial relationship with God, but he does so as their pastor. It is because God is their Father that his disciples need not be anxious about any aspect of life (Matt. 6:25-31); 'your heavenly Father knows' (Matt. 6:32). Because the sovereign God is their Father, they can be assured that he will provide for all their needs. They are family.

A new family

In the New Testament only Paul uses the language of adoption. However, the idea of belonging to the family of God is present throughout the New Testament. We read in John 1:12-13, 'to all who did receive him [Jesus], who believed in his name, he gave the right to become children of God, who were born, not of blood nor of the will of the flesh nor of the will of man, but of God'. Later in the same Gospel, Jesus tells Nicodemus, 'the teacher of Israel', that 'unless one is born again he cannot see the kingdom of God' (John 3:3). A new birth into a new family is necessary for anyone to see and enter the kingdom of God (John 3:5-6). In his first letter John writes, 'See what kind of love the Father has given to us, that we should be called children of God; and so we are' (1 John 3:1).

The privilege of our adoption

Being a Christian is about belonging to a family whose Father is God and whose Saviour and elder brother is God's own Son, Jesus Christ (Heb. 2:11). This is the Christian's highest and holiest privilege. Because we are his children, his adopted sons in Christ, we have unfettered access into God's presence. We are urged to come with confidence to the throne of God's grace (Heb. 4:16). We are assured that God, who is our Father, will supply all our needs 'according to his riches in glory in Christ Jesus' (Phil. 4:19). And Jesus himself tells us that we need not be anxious about our daily needs in life because 'your heavenly Father knows that you need them all' (Matt. 6:32).

The privilege of adoption reaches its highest height in Paul's affirmation that God's children, his adopted sons, are 'heirs of God and fellow heirs with Christ, provided we suffer with him in order that we may also be glorified with him' (Rom. 8:17).

It is almost impossible to unpack what Paul writes. The thought is so rich, so profound, so 'out of this world'. This last phrase echoes what the apostle John wrote: 'See what kind of love the Father has given to us, that we should be called children of God; and so we are' (1 John 3:1). The phrase 'what kind of love' could be translated, 'from what country is this love'. John is marvelling at the 'out of this world' character of God's love in making judgment-deserving sinners his children.

'Heirs of God and fellow [or joint] heirs with Christ ... provided we suffer with him'. The great privilege of adoption into God's family as his beloved sons carries with it the privilege of suffering 'with' Christ. Christians suffer 'for' Christ, for his cause and honour and kingdom. But this suffering is also 'with' Christ.

The responsibility of our adoption

Belonging to a family brings responsibilities. For the Christian, belonging to God's family in Christ means that we are called to reflect the 'family likeness'. God's ultimate purpose is to conform all his children into the likeness of his Son (Rom. 8:29). This will mean, among other things, having the same attitude to sin as the Lord Jesus Christ had. Never once did Jesus capitulate to temptation, in his thoughts or in his actions. He always did his Father's will and kept all of his commandments. Similarly, all Christians are summoned to 'be perfect, as your heavenly Father is perfect' (Matt. 5:48).

This is a note Paul highlights in Romans 8. He tells us that 'all who are led by the Spirit of God are sons of God' (Rom. 8:14). This idea of being 'led by the Spirit' is much misunderstood. In the previous verse Paul had written, 'if by the Spirit you put to death the deeds of the body, you will live'. Then he continues: 'For all who are led by the Spirit of God are sons of God.' The key word is *'For'*. Paul is telling the church in Rome that one of the marks of a son of God is that he will seek actively and daily, with the help or the leading of the Spirit, to put sin to death in his body. The Holy Spirit's new covenant ministry in the children of God is to sanctify them and make them increasingly like Christ. He does this by producing in his children a new resolve to say 'No' to sin (Titus 2:12 NIV). Because he is the *Holy* Spirit, he cannot but work in us to make us holy as God is holy (1 Pet. 1:15). Without his indwelling presence and help we could never put sin to death. But with his promised help, there is no sin that we cannot refuse, resist, and even kill.

How does he help us to do this? He does this principally by bringing to bear on our lives the virtue of the Saviour who died to sin and rose in newness of life (Rom. 6:1-11).

We noted earlier that a Christian is someone who has been united to Jesus Christ. The Jesus to whom all Christians have been united, died to the ruling power of sin and rose in triumph over sin's stronghold of death. He is our sin-conquering, Satan-defeating Saviour. In ourselves we do not have the resources to resist and overcome Satan's carefully devised temptations. But 'in Christ' we are 'more than conquerors' (Rom. 8:37). It is the Holy Spirit, as the Spirit of Christ, who gives us the help we need to 'put to death the deeds of the body', that is, the sins that find expression through our bodies. John Owen captured this truth memorably:

> Set faith at work on Christ for the killing of thy sin. His blood is the great sovereign remedy for sin-sick souls. Live in this, and thou wilt die a conqueror; yea, thou wilt, through the good providence of God, live to see thy lust dead at thy feet.[1]

---

[1] John Owen, *Works*, (London: Banner of Truth Trust, 1966), VI:79.

This is the leading of the Holy Spirit. As the Spirit of Christ he leads us to do battle with sin and to put sin to death in our lives. In this he acts also as the 'Spirit of adoption' (Rom. 8:15). There is a developing, unfolding sequence in Paul's teaching in Romans 8:13-17. Our status as sons of God is confirmed by us being led by the Spirit to put sin to death. The Spirit who leads us to kill the sin that yet remains in us leads us in this gospel warfare to 'cry, "Abba! Father!"' (Rom. 8:15). The verb '*cry*' points, not to an experience of calm reflection, but to an experience of inner agony. The same word is used to describe Jesus' cry on the cross. It is in the Christian's Spirit-led combat with sin that he cries, 'Father!' This 'cry' is a mark of 'family belonging'. It is a genuine family identifier.

This new covenant ministry of the Holy Spirit in the Christian belongs to his ministry of 'replication' (the word is Calvin's). The image he first forged in Christ he comes to replicate in believers. Every believer has been predestined to be conformed to Christ's likeness 'in order that he [Christ] might be the firstborn among many brothers' (Rom. 8:29). This is the ultimate reason why God adopts men and women, boys and girls, into his family.

God's salvation is indeed a rescue mission. We are all in the greatest need of being rescued from the guilt and power of sin, and from the dark dominion of the devil (Col. 1:13). But God's salvation is more embracive. His ultimate purpose is to renew this fallen creation and restore it under the lordship and dominion of the Lord Jesus Christ (Eph. 1:10). Under Christ's lordship God's people live as his brothers and sisters, rejoicing in the pre-eminence that their Saviour and elder brother possesses by his work of redemption (Phil. 2:9-11).

12

Salvation:
Jesus and Resurrection

Jesus' resurrection from the dead on the third day belongs to the heart of God's salvation as much as does his sin-atoning death on the cross. In his letter to the Romans, Paul declares that God's saving righteousness belongs to those who 'believe in him who raised from the dead Jesus our Lord, who was delivered up for our trespasses and raised for our justification' (Rom. 4:25).

For the early church, Jesus' resurrection was not simply a supernatural fact to rejoice in and proclaim; it was understood to lie at the very heart of the gospel. In 1 Corinthians 15, Paul dwells at length on the centrality of Christ's resurrection to the Christian faith. He begins the chapter by affirming that the resurrection belongs to the gospel truths of 'first importance' (1 Cor. 15:3-4). He proceeds to highlight the historicity of the event by referring to the many witnesses who bore testimony to the fact of Jesus' bodily resurrection on the third day (1 Cor. 15:5-8).

He then affirms with great vigour that 'if Christ has not been raised, then our preaching is in vain and your faith is in vain' and 'if in this life only we have hoped in Christ, we are of all people most to be pitied' (1 Cor. 15:14, 19).

But Christ's resurrection from the dead was not a doubtful or dubious fact; rather it was an undeniable fact: 'Christ has been raised from the dead' (1 Cor. 15:20). The Scriptures had foretold it (1 Cor. 15:4) and the many eye-witnesses had affirmed it (1 Cor. 15:5-8).

What then was the saving significance of Jesus' resurrection? What did Paul mean when he wrote that Jesus was 'raised for our justification' (Rom. 4:25)?

First, the resurrection was a vindication of who Jesus was and what he had accomplished. It confirmed that Jesus' death on the cross was a triumph, not a defeat:

> this Jesus, delivered up according to the definite plan and foreknowledge of God, you crucified and killed by the hands of lawless men. God raised him up, loosing the pangs of death, because it was not possible for him to be held by it (Acts 2:23-24).

In raising his Son from the dead, God the Father was placarding to the cosmos the triumph of the crucified Christ.

Second, the resurrection was a declaration by God that Jesus was 'the Son of God in power' (Rom. 1:4). The resurrection did not in any way make Jesus the Son of God; he was eternally God the Son (John 1:1-4). But the resurrection 'declared' to the world that he was the Son of

God 'in power', crucified in weakness but now living by the 'power of God' (see 2 Cor. 13:4).

It is possible, however, that we should translate the Greek word *horisthentos* ('declared' ESV) in Romans 1:4 as 'appointed' or 'constituted'. Paul is not saying that Jesus only became, was 'appointed', the Son of God at his resurrection. This is clear from what we read in verse 3 and later in 8:32. The gospel concerns 'his Son', the Son the Father did not spare but delivered up for us all. It was his own Son that the Father delivered up for us on Calvary's cross. It was this eternal Son who was 'appointed Son of God in power by his resurrection from the dead according to the Spirit of holiness'.

The contrast Paul is making in Romans 1:3-4 is between the 'two successive stages' of the Lord's earthly life. Paul is not saying there was a time when Jesus was not the Son of God and another when he is. No, he is the Son of God both in his humiliation and in his exaltation. But in his humiliation Jesus' eternal Sonship was marked by weakness. In his risen exaltation his Sonship is marked by 'the Spirit of holiness'.

Third, the resurrection secured our justification (Rom. 4:25). Is this not surprising? Does this not appear to conflict with what Paul writes in Romans 3:24, that we are justified by God's grace as a gift 'through the redemption that is in Christ Jesus'; and what he says in Romans 5:9, that we are 'justified by his [Christ's] blood'? If it was the sin-bearing, sin-atoning death of Christ that justifies us, and this justification comes to us from the grace of God, and is received by us through faith alone (Rom. 3:27-28; 4:1-8), what can Paul mean in Romans 4:25? In particular, what does the word '*for*' (*dia* in Greek) mean?

We first must say that without the resurrection, the cross would have been an unmitigated tragedy (1 Cor. 15:3-4, 14, 17; Rom. 6:4-5). Jesus' death and resurrection are seen in the New Testament essentially to be one event, two halves of the one whole, which is Paul's point in Romans 4:25. Consider the following:[1]

(1) Only as the 'living' Lord can Jesus be the object of faith. Saving faith is directed to the Saviour who rose on the third day and now reigns at the right hand of his Father. This is why Christians who are faithful to the Bible's teaching do not fix their thoughts (far less their jewellery!) on a crucified Christ, but on a risen, living, reigning Lord. He '*was*' delivered up for our trespasses, but '*now*' he ever lives to make intercession for us (Heb. 7:25; 9:24).

(2) It is in union with Christ that we are justified (Rom. 8:1), and that union is with the risen and reigning Saviour.

(3) The righteousness of Christ by which we are justified is the righteousness of the risen, living Christ (1 Cor. 1:30). He was 'obedient to the point of death' and in consequence 'God has highly exalted him and bestowed on him the name that is above every name, so that at the name of Jesus every knee should bow, in heaven and on earth and under the earth, and every tongue confess that Jesus Christ is Lord,

---

[1] See John Murray, *The Epistle to the Romans* (Marshall, Morgan and Scott, 1967), pp. 156-157.

to the glory of God the Father' (Phil. 2:8-11).

(4) The death and resurrection of Christ are inseparable. Christ's death could have no efficacy for us in isolation from his resurrection. We must always distinguish Jesus' death and resurrection, but never separate them.

(5) It is through the mediation of the risen Saviour that we come into the grace of acceptance with God (Rom. 5:2). When we rightly think of Jesus' 'finished work', the finished work of making atonement for sin, we must never forget his 'continuing work' as our interceding Mediator at his Father's right hand.

The resurrection is not only the public seal and sign of our Saviour's victory over sin, death, and Satan, but it belongs to the essence of our salvation. We are saved and justified and sanctified and ultimately glorified by the risen Lord Jesus Christ. The resurrection assures us that his death actually has benefits. We share in those benefits because of his resurrection (Rom. 6:4-5).

13

Salvation's Ultimate Purpose: Christ Over All

S alvation is not supremely about individuals finding peace with God and the hope of glory—though it is about that. The Bible's teaching on salvation transcends the individual and embraces the whole creation. The apostle Paul writes about this in his letter to the Romans:

> the creation waits with eager longing for the revealing of the sons of God. For the creation was subjected to futility, not willingly, but because of him who subjected it, in hope that the creation itself will be set free from its bondage to decay and obtain the freedom of the glory of the children of God (Rom. 8:19-21).

Just as Adam's sin brought the whole creation into a state of rebellion, futility, and corruption, so in Jesus Christ the whole creation will be restored (and more than restored!) to its original pristine purity.

In his letter to the Ephesians Paul writes about God fulfilling his eternal plan 'to unite all things in him [Christ], things in heaven and things on earth' (Eph. 1:10). Here Paul brings together God's proximate and ultimate purpose in salvation. His proximate purpose is to save a world of lost, judgment-deserving sinners by uniting them to his Son, Jesus Christ. 'In Christ' and 'in him' are Paul's most frequently used descriptions of a Christian. But God has a more ultimate purpose in saving sinners. That ultimate purpose is to make his Son the head of a new heavens and a new earth. Most English translations miss the specific point Paul is making. Verse 10 could better be translated, 'to sum up again under one head …'

The Bible has a breathtaking panoramic understanding of redemption. God's redeeming work in Christ transcends rescuing sinners from their bondage to sin and Satan. There is, therefore, a developing, or unfolding, connection between Ephesians 1 verse 7 and verses 8-10. God's redeeming work in Christ embraces the totality of the cosmos. The redeeming grace that God has 'lavished upon us, in all wisdom and insight', has a more ultimate end in view than the redemption of individual sinners. What God in the gospel of redeeming grace makes known to us is nothing less than 'the mystery of his will'.

A gospel mystery

A gospel 'mystery' is not a truth that remains an insoluble puzzle. It is, rather, a truth that we could never know unless God in his grace reveals it to us. The word '*mystery*' appears seventeen times in Paul's letters, seven times in Ephesians (1:9; 3:3, 4, 6, 9; 5:32; 6:19). The gospel is nothing less than the revealed plan and purpose of God for his glory and for bringing justified and sanctified sinners to share in his glory (Rom. 5:2; 8:17). Paul speaks of 'the mystery of Christ, which was not made known to the sons of men in other generations as it has now been revealed to his holy apostles and prophets by the Spirit. This mystery is that the Gentiles are fellow heirs, members of the same body, and partakers of the promise in Christ Jesus through the gospel' (Eph. 3:4-6) The unity of Gentiles and Jews in 'the same body' is a prelude to and a foretaste of the cosmic unity that Paul highlights in Ephesians 1:10.

The mystery that God has revealed (1:9) is his 'plan for the fullness of time, to unite all things in him [Christ], things in heaven and things on earth' (1:10). When Adam sinned, God's good creation was defaced. Sin came into the world (Rom. 5:12). Satan became the god of this world (2 Cor. 4:4). The whole world came under the diabolical rule of the enemy of our souls (1 John 5:19). The whole creation is presently in 'bondage to corruption' and waits to 'obtain the freedom of the glory of the children of God' (Rom. 8:21). Adam's sin was a cosmic tragedy. But God already had a 'purpose', and that purpose was to unite all things in Christ, 'things in heaven and things on earth'. Paul makes a similar statement in his letter to the Colossians, where he speaks of God through Christ reconciling to himself 'all things, whether on earth or in heaven, making peace by the blood of his cross' (Col. 1:20). The whole creation that was 'lost' to God through the fall will be restored to God through Christ.

Paul uses a vivid verb in Ephesians 1:10 to capture the glorious cosmic unity that God is in the process of accomplishing in Christ. The ESV translates it, 'to unite all things in him'; the NIV (2011), 'to bring unity to all things ... under Christ'; the KJV, to 'gather together in one all things in Christ'; the NASV, 'the summing up of all things in Christ'. The verb appears in only one other place in the New Testament, Romans 13:9, where Paul says that God's commandments are 'summed up in this word: "You shall love your neighbour as yourself."' It is clear that the verb contains the idea of 'gathering together and bringing into a unity'.

The context, however, suggests another way to translate this Greek compound. In Ephesians 1:22, Paul tells us that the Father has given Christ as 'head over all things'. A better translation might be, 'to be head *again* over all things'. Creation has a 'head', who is Jesus Christ. Paul is telling the Ephesians that God's purpose 'which he set forth in Christ' is 'to head up again all things in him'. Before Adam's rebellion, God's Son was the 'head' of creation. The triune God's lordship of creation was mediated through the Son. God's ultimate purpose, then, is to re-establish the Son as the head of creation.

It is imperative that we understand that God's purpose in salvation does not ultimately focus on us, but on his Son. Paul makes this explicit in Romans 8:29: 'For those whom he foreknew he also predestined to be conformed to the image of his Son, in order that he might be the firstborn among many brothers.' The ultimate cosmic glory of the

Son is the Father's pre-eminent purpose in redeeming sinners. If nothing else, this should teach us that our blessedness is tied to Christ's exaltation as head over all things. Modern evangelicalism has often been infiltrated, even scarred, by the self-centredness of modernity. It is as if God exists to make our lives complete. God's purpose is indeed to make our lives complete, but that completeness is bound up with the cosmic triumph of our head, Jesus Christ.

Creation has a God-ordained *telos* or ultimate object or aim. One day every knee will bow and every tongue confess that Jesus Christ is Lord (Phil. 2:9-11). Jesus will be in the midst of God's throne (Rev. 7:17). He will make all things new (Rev. 21:5). He will wipe away every tear from our eyes. Death will be no more. There will be no more mourning or crying or pain, 'for the former things [will] have passed away' (Rev. 21:4). The promise God made to Abraham so many years before, that he would be his and his offspring's God, will come to its climactic fullness: 'He will dwell with them, and they will be his people, and God himself will be with them as their God' (Rev. 21:3); and God will be all in all (1 Cor. 15:28). 'Amen. Come, Lord Jesus!' (Rev. 22:20).

History is going places—somewhere very special!

For Further Reading

Where to start

Sinclair B. Ferguson, *The Christian Life* (Banner of Truth Trust, 2013).

J. I. Packer, *God's Words* (Inter-Varsity Press, 1981).

J. C. Ryle, *Holiness* (Banner of Truth Trust, 2014).

In more detail

John Murray, *Redemption Accomplished and Applied* (Banner of Truth Trust edit. by permission of Wm B. Eerdmans, 2016).

Richard B Gaffin, *Resurrection and Redemption* (P & R Publishing, 1987).

Westminster Confession of Faith (Banner of Truth Trust, 2018).

Chad Van Dixhoorn, *Confessing the Faith* (Banner of Truth Trust, 2014,)

Emily Van Dixhoorn, *Confessing the Faith: Study Guide* (Banner of Truth Trust, 2017).

The bigger picture

John Calvin, *The Institutes of the Christian Religion* (1541 edit., tr. Robert White, Banner of Truth Trust, 2014;

1559 edit., tr. Ford Lewis Battles, Westminster Press, 1960).

John Murray, *The Epistle to the Romans* (Marshall, Morgan and Scott, 1967).

B. B. Warfield, *The Plan of Salvation* (Simpson Publishing, 1997).